David Reid

The Digital Broker's Playbook
A Guide to Modernizing Your Insurance Agency
© 2021 by David Reid
All Rights Reserved

ISBN 978-1-63676-

No part of this book may be reproduced, stored in a retrieval system, or transmitted by any means without the written permission of the author and publisher.

Printed in the United States of America
1 2 3 4 5 6 7 8 9

THE DIGITAL BROKER'S PLAYBOOK

A Guide to Modernizing Your Insurance Agency

Contents

Contents

Introduction

When I was an insurance broker, a typical day might look something like this: I have a fifteen-employee group, and I'm re-enrolling their medical, dental, and life insurance. I go to my storeroom and I grab fifteen medical forms, fifteen dental forms, and fifteen life forms. I collate them, type a memo, and after that, I hop in my car, drive across town, and walk in to physically deliver them to the group. I then follow up with their administrator every few days. "Are the forms done? No? Okay, I'll call again later."

The next call would go something like this: "Are the forms done yet? No? I understand that you're busy. We've just really got to get these forms done." Finally, once the group administrator gives me the green light, I once again hop in my car, drive across town, and pick up the forms. After I've checked in on my group and exchanged pleasantries, it's back into my car, where I traverse once more across town and make my way back to the office. I spend half a day proofing the paper forms. By the time I am done, I am practically seeing double. I inventory all the missing information, cross-referencing and double-checking as I go. Remember, I'm a broker, so perfectly proofing a stack of forms is not something I'm great at.

Then, I spend the next several days calling employees to gather their missing information. Sometimes, I get lucky and an employee picks up the first time I call; more often than not, that's not the case. Finally, once I have tracked down all of the missing bits and pieces, I finish completing all the forms, and individually fax completed forms to the insurance carrier.

Hopefully, none of the missing information involves signatures. If I'm missing a signature, it's a choice between signing a form for the employee or driving back to get it. Or, I can fax the form but, of course, that is a HIPAA violation unless the employee has a private fax.

If you're an insurance broker today and this is still how you do your job, you've got a big problem. This manner of operating is neither scalable nor sustainable. The world has evolved through the advent of technology-based solutions, and for the average broker today, those changes are impacting the way groups expect to do business. If a broker cannot keep up and offer new, digital solutions, they risk not only being unable to win new business, but losing a significant portion of their book of business as well. But there is enormous opportunity for brokers who make the switch from paper to digital, as long as they do it now—before their groups start looking around for a broker who can offer them the technology solutions they need to operate effectively today.

Emergence of Digital Brokers

My business partner, Courtney Guertin, and I started Ease with the mission to provide best-in-class technology solutions to small and medium-sized brokers. With this mission as our North Star, Ease is now well on our way to being the most widely adopted solution in the market.

As a broker myself, I've done it all—from enrollment meetings at five in the morning, just as the night shift was ending, to being holed up in a tiny conference room for the entire weekend (or for several weekends) during Open Enrollment season. I've taken my own wallet out to pay the rent for my business, and I've used credit cards to make payroll. I imagine that if you are an industry veteran like me, you can relate to some, if not all, of this. The brokers who have turned to Ease as their technology solution are the ones who can relate most to this way of operating—indeed, they are the ones with the most to gain from partnering with Ease.

The past ten years have brought some of the biggest changes to the insurance landscape we've seen in the previous several decades combined. The popularity of cloud-based software in everyday life, the mass adoption of Zoom during the COVID-19 pandemic, and the growing number of Millennials—the children of the Baby Boomers who make up a massive demographic group, and grew up with this cloud-based software—have dramatically shifted the needs of small businesses across the country. The relationships that were the foundation of our industry have been called into question as Millennials begin to ascend into leadership positions within HR and finance, as well as start their own businesses. Unlike their predecessors, these new decision-makers will demand that their HR teams and employees have access to the necessary tools to make benefits enrollment easier. They expect digital portals and online applications. They don't want—and truthfully, will no longer tolerate—a massive pile of paper forms, which means that brokers who still operate with paper are already—and surely will continue—losing customers.

It's critical, however, to keep in mind that these are still small businesses and that they make decisions differently from large companies. When you're talking to small business owners about making any kind of purchase, their mind goes to how that cost will immediately and directly affect their paycheck and their wallet.

Evolving Needs

So, what do employer groups—particularly small businesses—want from you, their broker?

- They want a technology solution that will solve the time drain and pain points of manual benefits administration.
- They want a benefits package that is customizable, based on varied and diverse employer and employee needs.
- They want to have a suite of resources available around the clock to manage benefits, onboarding, and the entire universe of their HR systems and processes.

The good news for you is that of that list, the one that is hardest to fill is the second—the custom benefits package—because while the other two can be easily bought, tailoring benefits to a variety of employees requires expertise. This can become your key differentiator.

Most importantly, their broker has *trusted advisor* status. Business owners who prefer to work with people they like and trust. Someone who will take their call and feel their pain.

I know from experience that, as a whole, we brokers have been a little slow to adopt technology; however, in today's environment, there is simply no way to avoid it. I'll probably repeat this more than once in the following pages, but there is going to be an enormous wave of small and medium-sized businesses embracing technology over the next few years, and once they do, they will never look back. If you're a broker and those businesses are your customers, you want to be riding that wave, not find yourself being crushed beneath it.

Changing the Landscape

My dream to build a solution that would help brokers first emerged twenty years ago, perhaps even earlier; in the following pages, I will share a little about my personal background, where I come from, and how I got my start. I've always been wired to work hard; I suppose that I've always been entrepreneurial, but it has never been by design. Looking back, I wasn't always determined to start a business. And while I may have started out in my career unsure about where I might wind up, in looking today at what I do and the vital impact Ease has had on others, I think I truly have the best job in the world. I love this industry and I believe that good brokers provide an invaluable service to their customers. The initial vision that Courtney and I had for Ease is now flourishing, and that means that we are helping many, many brokers successfully infuse technology into their businesses.

My journey has enabled me to help thousands of agencies convert from paper to digital, as well as to help launch new agencies that are built on a digital foundation. As a result, these new digital brokers have grown by identifying areas to increase commissions that simply weren't possible before without the use of cloud-based software. What's more, their customers are even more likely to stick with them in the future, having navigated the digitalization of their HR processes together, rather than having to figure it out alone. They've secured their future, making their books more attractive to potential acquisition and cutting down on paper use.

The clock is ticking. If you're a broker who is still tied to paper and you believe it's just too late—or just too difficult—to switch to the digital playbook, please keep reading. It isn't too late and it's much easier than you think. This book will show you how.

Part 1

Becoming a Broker

I grew up in South St. Paul, Minnesota. Though today the Twin Cities have a reputation of being dynamic and modern, things looked very different when I was growing up in my Twin City suburb back in the 1960s. The area that I lived in was one of the least advantaged communities; it was a predominantly blue-collar town, and most of my friends' dads worked in the stockyards or meat-packing plants at some point. This socioeconomic backdrop colored much of my young worldview and affects me still today. I've seen the intrinsic value of putting in a hard day's work, of getting your hands dirty, and of making something that improves the lives of others.

While many, if not most, of my social circle was raised experiencing some level of economic hardship, my experience was unique, in that my dad was a doctor, our town's general practitioner. In many ways, I can attribute my work ethic and my zeal for helping others back to my dad. I remember hopping in the car and riding along with him when he would get called to the hospital, a pint-sized co-pilot, quietly alongside for the mission. Growing up, it seemed that everyone knew my dad. In fact, he had personally delivered many of my friends.

Even though my family was considered very financially well off compared to most others in our town, that never affected the way I saw my father interact with our friends and neighbors. While I struggled at times in my adolescence with feeling that others viewed our family as a little bit different, I never saw my dad demonstrate anything other than compassion and kindness for the citizens of our town that counted on him to deliver their care.

My dad passed away unexpectedly when I was just nine years old. As our family navigated this season of grief, my mom stepped into the role of both parents. I was the youngest of five children, with my oldest sister being eighteen years older than myself. With several of my siblings being adults themselves when we lost our father, I think I felt compelled to grow up more quickly. I saw the way that my mom carried so much on her shoulders, and I think that it instilled in me a desire to work much earlier than had tragedy not struck our family. My mom was very active in the Ladies Auxiliary to the Veterans of Foreign Wars (VFW). She had been the president of the Auxiliary when my father passed away. And through her strength, grace, and determination, she later went on to work in politics for a US senator from Minnesota.

Loss will shape you regardless of how hard you try to prevent it. I emerged from the grief of my father's loss as someone more resilient, someone with a strong work ethic, and perhaps as a nod to my late dad, someone whose work needed to make a difference.

Whether through necessity or by design, I discovered early on that I loved to work. I started my first real job when I was just thirteen years old. Though I've tried my hand at many things—especially at a young age—one thing has always remained the same: Starting with that first job, and in every job since, I've always been selling something.

My first job was soliciting donations for the Lions Club. Not necessarily the most glamorous position, my chief responsibility (my only responsibility, truth be told) was to sit on the phone all day and call people. Since I was only thirteen at the time, I had to lie about my age just to get my foot in the door. After the initial job interview, we were sent to a conference room where I learned my quick pitch: "Hello, I'm David Reid with the Lions Club. We do this and this and that for the community and I'm hoping you will contribute $25 today . . ." Then we were sent to the call room where I was given an empty chair and told to start making calls. Every hour someone came around to check our progress. If you weren't bringing in enough donations, you were fired then and there. The stakes seemed high—even for a thirteen-year-old—but in spite of the sink-or-swim approach, I found that I was actually able to produce where others struggled. The approach was not at all what I had expected. But sales, it turned out, came naturally and I was very good at it.

When I was sixteen, I took another job that presented an opportunity for both more money and more responsibility. Husnicks Home Food Service was a family-owned business in my hometown of St. Paul. The specialty market delivered canned and frozen foods directly to people's homes. I was hired to make appointments for Husnicks, but I discovered that I was also very good at selling their food program. When I would speak to someone about setting an appointment for home delivery, I couldn't help but try to maximize the opportunity. Without ever intending to, I found myself contributing to sales off the side of my desk. So when Husnicks opened a new office in West St. Paul, I was offered the opportunity to manage it.

At sixteen years old, I found myself managing a half-dozen people—all phone sales representatives—and being responsible for all decisions around hiring and firing. Most kids my age were preoccupied with thoughts about Friday's football game or getting up the nerve to ask someone to the big dance. Instead, I spent my spare time thinking about how to coach my sales team to achieve their numbers, or if I was going to be able to quickly find the right person for that newly open position I had listed in the paper the week before. It was by no means a traditional start to my career, nor a traditional way to spend the latter part of my adolescence, but the lessons it afforded me have lasted a lifetime.

There is a phrase that has been popularized in recent years, particularly when talking about some of the less traditional approaches to employment Millennials have taken. It's called "side hustle," and it speaks to anything and everything you can do outside of your day job to earn extra income. Long before this was a pop-culture phenomenon, it was my way of dipping my toe in the water of entrepreneurship. Before even graduating college, I had started my own business venture. I named my company DAR, which stood for

David A. Reid, International, and much like my moniker, the concept was very straightforward—I bought and sold products, such as insulated and vinyl can wraps, to put around beer cans. I would purchase a supply of the can wraps and then send sales prospecting letters and product samples to all the local liquor stores. If a store manager was interested, I'd drive over and deliver the wraps to the store.

Reflecting back on those early days, it's safe to conclude that I've always been more comfortable with being busy than with standing still. It's true that, even now, I don't like feeling idle, and my days are usually full from early morning until I lay my head down at night. That fullness can take several forms, undulating between being full of ideas to days or weeks being full of activity in an effort to make those ideas come to life. This has been the case for me from my earliest days, and suppose it could be summed up by simply saying that I've just always been entrepreneurial. I like to build things, whether it's a sales plan or a business or a thriving company culture. I think, like my late father, I am wired that when others see a problem, I have the lens to see an opportunity, a solution. The hard, roll-up-your-sleeves and get-your-hands-dirty work of solving the problem and figuring out the necessary steps to get to the desired result—that has always been the most fulfilling work to me. Problem, opportunity, solution.

Becoming a Broker

When I was preparing to graduate from college, I had decided that I wanted to be a stockbroker. Truthfully,

I was a little fuzzy on what exactly stockbrokers did; however, it seemed like a natural fit for a hardworking self-starter like me—someone eager to make his mark. I applied for a job at Continental Brokerage, thinking that it was a stock brokerage. However, when I arrived for the interview, I was surprised to learn that it was actually an insurance brokerage. I knew nothing about insurance, but the interview went well and, frankly, the job sounded appealing. When I was presented with an offer at the end of the interview, I made the leap and decided to take it.

In some ways, my job was not unlike many of the early sales positions I had held before. I called on insurance brokers to sell small group health insurance through John Alden. My job was to be on the phone with the brokers and represent John Alden. Insurance brokers were getting calls and quotes from lots of other reps, like Prudential, Guardian, United, etc. I'd send the brokers the quote for John Alden and then the challenge was to follow up and make sure my quote compared favorably with those from the other insurance reps. Much of my days consisted of: "Did you receive my proposal? How does it look? Who are we up against? Exactly how does our quote compare?"

I was quick and thorough and this helped me to sell a lot of insurance for the company. But as I performed, I also learned how the business worked. Even though I wasn't a broker myself then, I started to understand their job too. I was successful in my role at Continental, but I was ambitious and found myself wanting to move up.

After some time at John Alden, I got a call from a recruiter about a position with Lincoln National.

Lincoln was a very large insurance company, somewhat like Financial is today. The position there was similar to what I was doing for John Alden; however, it would grant me the opportunity to move into the larger group space. Though the work would be similar, I could learn about underwriting the financials and work with brokers on larger cases. Previously, I had been working with brokers that were selling groups between two and thirty employees. What pushed me over the edge about the opportunity with Lincoln was that now I'd be selling to brokers with groups as large as five hundred to one thousand lives. That kind of opportunity for new learning and growth was too enticing to turn down.

Emerging Technology

At Lincoln, we carried laptops. Now, this was back in 1990 when laptops were very new and, particularly in the insurance world, considered a little exotic. Because they were still pretty rare, when I would pull mine out, people would say, "Wow, I've only ever seen those on television!" I felt fortunate to join a company that believed in investing in technology for their employees. I was in a somewhat unique position, in that I was already comfortable with computers. I was an early adopter of Apple products, as I had an Apple computer in college. I immediately recognized how much it helped in my work. For example, I participated in debate in college. If you were ever part of a debate team, you understand how important—and how labor intensive—evidence cards were in the preparations process. I found that using a computer rather than a typewriter to make my evidence cards made my life so much easier. Aside from being faster, it was exponentially cleaner—no more Wite-Out and messy corrections!

My zeal for technology became an important factor with one of the brokers I called on at Lincoln National. His name was Gary Wert and he indicated that he was impressed with my apparent adeptness and skill with technology. After an appointment one day, he walked me out and asked, "Have you ever thought about becoming a broker?" I felt a bolt of electricity as his words found me; not only had I thought about it—lately it had been all I had thought about. I knew that it was exactly what I wanted to do with my career. Just as quickly as my thoughts began to take flight, I was pulled back down to earth. I was loyal to my company and at that point, I didn't want to leave. So, I told him that I was happy where I was but that if the right opportunity came along, I'd certainly consider it.

That conversation replayed itself in my mind many times over the days and weeks that followed. I realized that I was ready to launch the next phase of my career. Not long after, I achieved my goal of becoming a broker, and Gary and I started working together. Being a broker came naturally to me. I loved the work, and found that I was actually quite good at it. After nine years of a strong partnership, Gary and I became partners. Our brokerage was widely known and well respected in Minneapolis. We initially called our new company Gary Wert and Associates, and later renamed it to Unison. At the time that I became a full partner, we had about twenty-five employees, a number that steadily continued to grow.

I learned many things from the years I spent working with Gary. He played an important role as a mentor at a pivotal stage of my career, and many of the skills I bring to my business today, I learned from him. Gary taught me what traits to look for when hiring new employees; from watching him, I learned how to best grow a team and lead them into stronger positions of leadership. Many of the fundamental principles about running a business, I first learned from Gary. I also learned then that positive business relationships were essential to my success. Rather than pursuing short-term gains at the cost of long-term relationships, I made certain not to ever make enemies or burn bridges. A competitor today might be an ally in the future.

In 1999, we started working with an early vendor in the online benefits enrollment space, Benefits Connect. I was very interested in the new technology, as I had already written a database application that our agency, along with a few others, had been using for quoting, managing contacts, workflow, and commission accounting. At the time, other vendors were pushing out online-capable programs, but since I had no formal training or skills in HTML, my application wasn't online.

Understanding the importance that technology could play in our space, we became the first broker customer of Benefits Connect and immediately started putting our groups online. It wasn't an overnight success, as the software could be unpredictable and connectivity was often a problem. Some of our groups would get frustrated by the long wait to change screens, particularly during peak time or busy seasons. Because this kind of technology was still so rare in our industry, when our groups would encounter some of these bumps along the way, many would express a desire to make the jump back to paper forms. The learning curve was considerably steep for some brokers, as well as for the administrative people working for them, who would often return from the training classes confused and discouraged.

Apprize

Sensing a need, Gary and I started a new company, Apprize Technology, in 2005. Our mission was singular and clear: to make brokers' lives easier by getting their groups to enroll and manage benefits online. Because our other company, Unison, was a brokerage, we had to create an entirely separate corporate entity to avoid competing with other brokers. Gary and I agreed that we would both own the two companies, and while Gary remained as the president of Unison, I would step into the role of president for Apprize. I let my broker's license lapse, because I felt it was important to not have my foot on both sides of the aisle; my integrity wouldn't allow me to operate as both a technology provider and a broker in my new role. I was all in on my new path.

There were many brokers who had purchased Benefits Connect but couldn't manage the new technology. Apprize was there to help get them up and running online. I was so excited about this new technology and how it had the potential to completely revolutionize a broker's job. I went out and began telling all our customers that they needed to be online immediately.

Unfortunately, I learned that not everybody shared my enthusiasm or wanted it as much as I did. I couldn't understand those who were content to rely on the old way of doing business, but there were plenty of brokers who were interested. I focused on them.

Gary Wert and I were bootstrappers, though we wouldn't have called ourselves that at the time. We didn't know anything about venture capital, and the way we grew our business was always out of our own pockets, never through investments or borrowed funds. Despite this conservative approach, in just two years' time, we went from a dead start to $1.8 million in revenue. What's more, this took place between 2005 and 2007, making our accomplishment that much more impressive, upon reflection. Even by Silicon Valley standards for a start-up today, this is considered quite a feat. Despite that, Gary and I didn't really see it as that impressive at the time, likely because we were investing money and spending it just as quickly as we were earning it. We were reinvesting back into the company as quickly as we could.

Apprize had a repetitive process that worked: it solved a relevant problem for a large marketplace and although it was new at the time, it wasn't completely foreign territory. But Apprize was designed for large groups of at least one hundred and, more typically, larger than five hundred employees. These large customers had complex benefits situations, while the majority of brokers were handling small groups that only needed a simple solution.

At that time, most brokers were typically handling ten-employee groups, which usually only had one or two medical plans. Everyone in the group had the same plan so it was very simple. They didn't need complex workflows and approval processes, numerous plan options, or multiple health care networks across different states. The reason many brokers were struggling was because the software was designed for large businesses, but didn't fit the needs of the average small business. It had no connection to the way they worked or the problems they were trying to solve. This realization was the idea that sparked the creation of Ease.

Ease

I decided to design a cloud-based application, like Salesforce or SAP, built to specifically help brokers bring their small businesses online, with a user interface that would make setting up a group extremely simple. My vision was that any skilled broker who knew the insurance industry would be able to use this application. I wanted to take what I'd learned from the other products I'd touched along the way and blueprint the minimum requirements for the largest segment of the market: small businesses. A good example of what I had in mind was QuickBooks. If you're a business owner, you don't really need lessons to begin using QuickBooks. Its user-centric functionality and design are intuitive for users at every level. In simple terms, everything you're looking at just makes sense to you. You know exactly what to do.

I met Courtney Guertin in Minnesota. Courtney worked for a software company as an engineer, and they built a lot of what they refer to as vertical CRMs,

Client Relationship Management programs, serving particular industries. He had experience working with a vertical CRM in the HRIS space and he really enjoyed it. In Minnesota, my company Unison, while not the biggest brokerage, was well known, particularly for being very tech forward. Back in the day, if you were in the tech industry and you were building a product used by brokers, there was a good chance that you would meet me pretty quickly; that's how I met Courtney. Early on, he did some work for us at Apprize, but not long afterwards, he moved out to Silicon Valley and co-founded Kiip, a mobile rewards company.

My vision to build a cloud-based application designed to specifically help brokers bring their small businesses online continued to intensify. When I was ready to build what I then called Enrollease, I found myself issuing requests for proposals to engineers I'd worked with over the years. Knowing I needed someone I could trust, I went to Courtney with these bids and asked him to help me select the engineer. Courtney was building his company Kiip, but agreed to help by working with me on nights and weekends. When we were ready, we launched a minimum viable product—meaning it had just enough features to satisfy early customers while providing feedback for future product development—and the contracts came very quickly.

Getting Ready to Launch

Because of my existing Apprize connections, we made the decision to launch in Minnesota when it came time for the product to go live. From July of 2012 until the fall of 2014, Courtney, myself, and Jon Orchard—who joined us early on—nurtured Enrollease tirelessly. Jon is the kind of guy who would take on any project, quickly learn what he needed to know, and could handle whatever came up. He was like our very own Swiss Army knife in those early days of bringing Ease to market.

By the fall of 2014, Enrollease was becoming too big for Courtney to manage on nights and weekends. By this time, we really believed that we could turn this into a competitive solution for SMBs across the country. Courtney began to work on Enrollease full-time, and it wasn't a moment too soon—the industry was just starting to heat up. A company called Zenefits launched, taking off like a tsunami. Founded by Parker Conrad, Zenefits received an investment of $78 million in 2014, and was rumored to be valued by Silicon Valley at $500 million within the first year of publicly offering their software.

Zenefits was cutting out the broker. Being a broker myself, I didn't just know a lot about brokers, I cared a lot about brokers too. And I knew something that Zenefits did not: employee benefits is a personal experience. And we believed, and still believe, that replacing the experience with technology isn't the right approach. We wanted to go in a very different direction by building excellent software specifically *for* brokers, and we were betting that brokers would recognize the benefits and make the transition. Courtney and I decided we were going to take on outside investment to enable us to go toe-to-toe with other solutions looking to replace brokers.

We made our first venture pitch in early February of 2015. Barely three weeks later, I was stepping out of a rented pickup truck and emptying my personal belongings into the back bedroom of our new offices in downtown San Francisco. In early March we closed the $2.1 million investment from Silicon Valley investors, hired our first two employees, and on September 17, 2015, we launched a new and improved solution—Ease Central—built using our learnings from Enrollease.

Part 2

Industry Changes: Big Risks and Big Opportunities

Demographic and market changes today are affecting the way small businesses operate, particularly in their HR department. These changes bring new risks for brokers, but they also can open you up to enormous opportunities. Guardian Life's Workplace Benefits Study discusses these changes in detail, and this chapter is based on their research.[1]

Small business HR priorities are increasingly focused on three primary areas: bringing in and keeping talented employees, especially Millennials; handling compliance issues; and keeping overall benefits costs down. In order to achieve these goals, the use of technology and outsourcing is a critical component. Technology offers a solution to all three of these problems, enabling them to satisfy the expectations of their employees and to increase their business efficiencies.

In addition, demographic changes have drastically altered both what employers and what their employees

---

[1] Guardian Life Insurance Company of America, 5th Annual Workplace Benefits Study, Small Business – Big Benefits and Game Changer: The Digitalization of Employee Benefits Delivery, 2017.

expect from the benefits experience. Millennials now make up more than half of the US labor force, according to the Guardian's research, and they are expected to represent 75% of American workers by 2025. This group demands an individualized and flexible benefits platform, and overwhelmingly we see from this group that it must also be digital and mobile. Millennial employers in particular want an easy, integrated system that allows their employees to access and monitor their own benefits anytime from anywhere.

POTENTIAL CHANGES TO BENEFITS ADMINISTRATION
Within the Next Three Years

Expand Cloud Applications	New Platform Software	Integrate More Functions	Plan to Outsource More
42%	39%	36%	27%

Industry analysts expect that small businesses turning to cloud-based systems and digitization of their processes will continue to skyrocket. Today, managing benefits programs is already difficult for employers, especially small businesses. Going forward, we will likely continue to see more shifts in healthcare policy and regulation as each new administration tries to address healthcare reform. Meanwhile, approximately 10,000 Baby Boomers retire each day,[2] aging into

---

[2] https://smartasset.com/retirement/baby-boomers-retiring

Medicare and leaving vacant roles that Millennials are assuming at a faster rate than any of their generational counterparts. Advancing technology is creating new opportunities while shifting employers' expectations. It's clear that the complexity of benefits administration will only grow. This means that small business owners will need more assistance than ever from their brokers to help develop and execute successful benefits strategies. Being able to offer technology advice and support can help you maintain your status as a trusted advisor and slams the door shut on other companies using these changes as an entry point. In the past, technology solutions in the benefits and HRIS space may have been viewed as "nice to have" rather than need to have. But following the life-changing events of COVID-19 in 2020 and the surge of virtual work environments, those same nice-to-have solutions transformed overnight into critical tools to empower virtual workforces.

According to the Guardian study, one in three small businesses include the outsourcing of benefits

OUTSOURCING IS HELPING CONTROL COSTS
% Strongly Agree Among Small Businesses

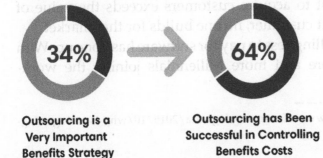

34%

64%

Outsourcing is a
Very Important
Benefits Strategy

Outsourcing has Been
Successful in Controlling
Benefits Costs

administration as part of their benefits strategy, with 30% increasing their outsourcing in the past few years.

As technology continues to advance, prices for technology drop while tech products get more advanced. According to the US Bureau of Labor Statistics, which tracks prices for numerous categories of goods over time, for the past eighteen years prices have steadily dropped in almost every tech sector.[3] What this means is that technology solutions—including those in the HR and benefits space—have become much more readily available and affordable for even the smallest firms, allowing these employers to abandon paper and adopt better, digital solutions. There are several factors that have helped drive down cost in this space, while driving up adoption:

- Implementation costs are down. The general public's proficiency with cloud-based software makes adoption easier. Bandwidth going up makes online training fast and cheap.
- Distribution costs are down. Businesses can research, buy, and implement entirely through the web! That means the cost to acquire a new SMB user is less than it once was, improving margins for businesses that build the software—if the cost to acquire customers exceeds the value of that customer, no one builds for that market.
- Willingness to pay for software has gone up. With more and more Millennials joining the work-

---

[3] https://www.weforum.org/agenda/2015/10/why-is-tech-getting-cheaper/

EMPLOYER ADOPTION OF HR TECHNOLOGY
% Using Systems/Software for Each Function

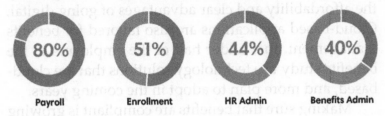

80%	51%	44%	40%
Payroll	Enrollment	HR Admin	Benefits Admin

force, recruiting and retaining them means representing your company well and tailoring your offerings to this technology-driven generation.

Industry analysts report that in addition to improving the employee experience, digitizing the benefits process can significantly improve employee productivity and efficiency. Guardian's study notes that employers who identify themselves as highly digital find much greater efficiency in record-keeping and enrollment in comparison with paper-based companies.

TECHNOLOGY IMPROVES HR SERVICE EXPERIENCE
% Highly Satisfied Among Small Businesses

	Highly Digital	More Paper-based
Payroll Processing	88%	66%
Benefits Administration	84%	50%
HR Administration	82%	52%

And while concerns about the cost of new technologies are a factor, they are increasingly outweighed by the affordability and clear advantages of going digital. Cloud-based applications are also favored for benefits management. Just under half of the employers in the benefits study use technology solutions that are cloud-based, and more plan to adopt in the coming years.

Making sure that benefits are compliant is growing increasingly more important, and research indicates that today, six in ten employers depend on their broker to help them manage these complexities. The Affordable Care Act, ACA adjustments with policy changes, global pandemic making tracking more difficult—our health care landscape places a heavy burden on employers, and finding the best solution means they need experienced guidance. Further, nine out of ten small businesses use a broker or advisor—with six in ten relying on a traditional broker for their other needs as well. If we agree that change is constant, you need a solution to manage change.

EMPLOYERS SEEK HELP WITH BENEFITS TECHNOLOGY

51% Half of All Employers Expect Their Broker to Recommend Innovative Benefits Technology Solutions.

The Guardian Study found that small businesses with an active broker typically offer their employees a broader array of insurance and benefits.

There is no question that the digital revolution has taken hold and is altering the way businesses, both large and small, make decisions and set priorities. And as this research clearly suggests, brokers who remain tied to the traditional, paper-based model are not only at grave risk of losing their groups to an advisor who offers digital solutions, but without question these brokers will face mounting difficulties in attracting new customers. But there is a massive opportunity here for brokers who have adopted technology solutions to take on an even more significant role in helping their groups navigate the many changes they will confront in the coming years.

Part 3

The New Players

Demographic shifts, technology adoption, and compliance management are some of the major threats and opportunities facing SMBs today. To tackle these challenges, business owners have a few models to choose from:

1. The first option is a familiar one. An employer partners with a broker, who then provides benefit consulting and helps them through the benefit selection process. Subsequently, the broker is compensated, in most cases, through the carrier. The broker also helps the employer choose, deploy, and manage technology solutions needed to facilitate benefit administration and other HR functions.

2. The next method is becoming increasingly more prevalent today. Software functions as the broker, meaning an employer selects their plans from a variety of options and handles benefits entirely themselves through the software. This places the burden entirely on the business owner. The software company is compensated by the carriers as though they were providing broker services.

3. The final model we'll discuss is that of the Professional Employment Organization (PEO). In these models, business owners purchase benefits and other services through a PEO, paying as much as $125 PEPM[4] for a variety of HR tools and services. PEOs are a different model entirely that emerged after the Affordable Care Act was put into place. Though this option is extremely costly, it has still gained momentum in recent years. Be advised, these PEOs are a very real threat to traditional brokers.

The second option listed above is what we refer to as Direct-to-Employer, or DTE—companies that sell software directly to SMBs receiving broker commissions directly from carriers without providing full broker services. One notable example of a DTE that made waves—until realizing that being a broker was a full-time job—is Zenefits.

Zenefits, lauded as one of the fastest-growing tech companies in history at one time, came in like a tidal wave, hitting the market hard and fast, and in a very visible way. It was founded by former CEO, Parker Conrad, in 2013. At the time, its business model was simple: give away HR software to businesses for free, but earn money via commissions that come from selling their group clients employee health insurance plans. They found a Trojan horse to cut brokers out of the equation completely. Parker has since left Zenefits and founded yet another company that competes with brokers, called Rippling. However, the model—and threat—of DTEs continues.

---

[4] https://www.gnapartners.com/lp/peo-pricing/

I am often invited to speak at conferences and events for brokers, my community. When I do, I typically incorporate a few slides and video clips from leaders of DTE companies so brokers know what our industry is up against. *These* are the wolves in sheep's clothing that you should be fearful of—and with good reason. Unlike yesterday's competitors, these DTEs have raised significant outside investment, it takes a lot to displace brokers after all, they've used that investment to drive exponential growth during a time of historic industry transformation, and, unlike the brokerage up the street, they are obsessed with growth—moving markets and taking advantage of the fact that agencies around the country have not talked to their groups about going online.

We brokers have historically been slower than some professions to embrace and adopt technology, and these DTEs and PEOs are not only aware of this tendency, but they have built an entire business model to take full advantage of that hesitancy. They have been very active in penetrating the market and going after your business. At Ease, we receive at least one call every day from an agency, frantically looking for an online solution because one of their clients is looking to switch to a DTE or PEO because of technology.

The fight for Millennials in the SMB HR and benefits space is well underway. These well-funded, technology-first competitors are using all the tools at their disposal to "disrupt" the role of the broker. And they're leading their sale with software. But in spite of this, most brokers today are still heavily reliant upon paper. Leaving the door open for these competitors, unlike the larger agency up the street, puts the industry at risk. Silicon Valley has invested hundreds of millions of dollars in solutions that cut brokers out of the equation. It's only a matter of time before these solutions get in touch with your groups.

Historically, the SMB benefits and HR space, particularly the micro-group with fewer than ten employees, has been ignored. Even though this represents 76% of employers, it has been seen as not profitable. After spending time in major cities like Los Angeles, I understand why. The process of delivering ten enrollment forms to a small company would take all day. In fact, some national agencies have built their business around buying large blocks of small group business and using technology as the way to make this segment profitable.

Profitability of small groups changes with technology because you no longer have to deliver forms. Not only that, the Millennial buyers don't necessarily expect as much face-to-face activity in their business relationships as long as their needs are met with an online solution. Combine this with two other factors:

1. Small group plans are "off the shelf" and generally do not require or allow any customization.
2. The compensation per employee per month is exponentially higher than with large groups.

All this means you can deliver a modern solution "at scale" and at a very low cost. Small group is now, if managed properly, the most lucrative segment of the group insurance market space. Here lies the reason major Silicon Valley investors have continually invested hundreds of millions of dollars into entities that possess an ability to displace the outdated broker.

A unifying fact about DTEs and PEOs is that they are both extremely proficient at digital marketing. They deploy clever tactics, like using publicly accessible data from platforms such as LinkedIn or Glassdoor to determine when a new employer has just surpassed the one hundred employee marker. They then pay for access to databases that allow them to stealthily acquire contact information, like phone numbers, for that employer. That information is fed into their CRM, like Salesforce, where sales reps begin their cold calling cadences and LinkedIn connection requests and their marketing teams begin their email campaigns. This process is well documented in the Silicon Valley software playbook *Predictable Revenue* by Aaron Ross and Marylou Tyler. From that point on, automated emails are then sent to the employers once a week, offering the DTEs software for free, or offering free trials of their payroll.

Unlike many traditional brokers who have resisted digital marketing or employing technology solutions for their groups, DTEs are highly versed in running online marketing campaigns and they leverage digital insights to help them win away your clients. These digital competitors rely heavily on email software capabilities to know exactly when during the day a prospective business owner opens their emails, what content they are reading, and what subject lines are driving them to click through to an action. All this data then helps your competitor know what offers are most relevant and enticing to a group, and thus triggers a direct call with a customized offer from one of their sales representatives.

Once a PEO or DTE has their foot in the door, they will not hold back. They use the publicly accessible databases, like miEdge, in order to see exactly which benefits you are offering your clients today. They can then use this data to layer on even more aggressive, more targeted digital ads. If the business owner visits the DTE's website to learn more, it will then initiate a series of retargeting ads, dangling an enticing free trial offer that will follow the employer around the internet until they click or follow through in some way.

The marketing power of these digital competitors is unlike anything you've experienced previously with another broker calling on your groups. DTEs and PEOs also capture customer information by prowling review sites such as G2.com and Capterra, and then target these very groups, showcasing their size and reputation, and positioning that they have customer referral programs that discount the employers' costs if they refer other businesses. For most brokers going up against a DTE or PEO on their own, it quickly begins to feel like a David and Goliath tale.

Another factor at work is what drives the DTE. Most brokers, to a large degree, approach this business as a "lifestyle" business. I've personally known many brokers that will look back at the early years where they had to work so many hours to build a book of business. Once established, the ongoing relationships with the business owners, combined with good service, allow them to maintain that business. There was less interest in continuing to work more hours—or for more money—than there was to enjoy a quality work/ life balance.

This thought process has nothing to do with the way a venture-funded DTE operates. Year-over-year (YOY) growth rates are expected to exceed 100% and the philosophy around work/life balance is that you "live to work" and you are measured to a "unicorn" standard. The leading investors in Silicon Valley won't even consider a company that has a business plan calling for less than a billion dollars of revenue.

There are a few interesting lessons that I've personally gleaned from watching companies like Zenefits or other DTEs go toe-to-toe with brokers. Unfortunately, the harsh reality is that customers are very hard to get, but they are very easy to lose. In the past, you and your competitors played in the same ecosystem, operating with similar resources and deploying similar mechanisms to keep and win business. Today, if you are competing against a DTE, a PEO, or a digital broker in general, you are no longer competing against someone playing at your level. It's like going from the minor league to the major league overnight. You may have had your clients for many years, but then a DTE comes along. Because they offer a particular tool that you don't have—payroll in this case—your customer decides to drop you and go with them. Solely relying on your relationship—with the shifts the industry has seen—is downright dangerous.

However, it is not all doom and gloom. Have you heard the expression, the sizzle sells the steak, but the steak is what keeps the customer coming back? It's one that I find myself saying a lot—especially when talking about PEOs and DTEs. There is a reason that this saying is particularly pertinent when talking about these types of competitors.

You see, Zenefits had the sizzle, but their steak turned out not to taste so good to the business they won, a problem that intensified as time wore on. Their experience didn't deliver against the many promises they made and, ultimately, the groups they won didn't keep going back to them. That means that fortunately, brokers like you are poised to win back against these commanding competitors if you can simply meet clients' technology expectations while delivering superior service.

It's important that you understand the nuances of the direct-to-employers that pose a real threat today. Zenefits' employee benefits experience couldn't match their promise. Others have had an approach that is a little different. Some DTEs will establish themselves by saying to the small business owner, "We are a modern payroll vendor. We are super easy to use and incredibly inexpensive. Just sign up today." The small business owner may then purchase them for payroll, thinking that is all they are signing up for. They then use a low-cost payroll as, what I would call, a backdoor entry. Once the DTE is in the room, they start to expand to fill the space, adding additional services sold through their software, including employee benefits, and peeling away your business as they go.

Consider this: in an average scenario, a typical small business may not have life insurance for its employees. That company's payroll vendor (in this case, the DTE) now has all the information they need to quote life insurance to that small business owner, because they already know the age of every employee, along with exactly how much money each person makes each year. The payroll vendor also knows the location of the business, the SIC code, the nature of the business, and can leverage private, expensive external data sources.

Where the payroll vendor already has the relevant customer's information that they need, a new insurance agent would typically have to gather information to generate a quote. The payroll vendor, on the other hand, already has all of that information and can just say, inside their software when the business owner of HR administrator logs in, "Hey, do you guys offer life insurance? No? Did you know for just $8.95 a month, you can offer coverage to all your employees? Want to learn more?" or "Just sign up right now, click here and say yes." The entire process is facilitated online and employees already have a login and are familiar with how their software works.

So, now the DTE might have that employer's business for payroll and life insurance. But they will not stop there. After that, they will then move on with a very frictionless approach to add disability insurance and flexible benefits. They'll repeatedly say, "See how nice this is when everything is in one place? Do you know that we can do the same thing with your medical plan? And what's more, it's free! You can start the process next time you run payroll, and we will do the rest for you." It's startlingly simple, and it doesn't stop there.

The employer just goes online and chooses their carrier from a drop-down menu on the DTE's system. Then they enter the current policy number and finally, very subtly, somewhere deep within the process, the business decision maker will need to sign some kind of agreement. Slipped in there will also be a broker of record letter agreement where the employer agrees to move the servicing agent over from you, their current broker, to the DTE. And just like that, they are in and you are out.

You can see why these DTEs have become very popular, and I would not be surprised to learn that you have lost a case to them if you are in one of their target markets, which is expanding rapidly. A significant part of their success is that they have figured out how to tap into the phenomena of a Millennial generation that expects everything to be available online. That's their core strength. Their weakness, which they wouldn't necessarily admit to as a weakness, is that they aren't—and don't want to be—brokers, in the sense we are accustomed to—everything is over the internet and the phone.

Don't expect options other than the most commonly used "off the shelf" products that are easy because they are simplistic, not necessarily the best for the customer. Creative, complex solutions that deliver results are only found in "broker land"—the place where brokers can easily win, and that advantage that should be exploited. Even if it is a Millennial customer, one that does not necessarily prioritize face-to-face service, they do favor expertise that delivers results. At the end of the day, *expertise* is what wins.

Over time, consistently demonstrating expertise leads to a trusted business relationship. You provide great service but they also trust your advice because they have come to know they can. This relationship, even if you are caught off guard from time to time, can save a case.

When I was a young broker, I remember one particular sales situation where I thought I was beating the incumbent broker really, really badly. I had the analysis, I had the savings. It was crystal clear to me and to the decision maker at the group that I had provided ideas and solutions that the company was likely going to implement because they made sense. From my perspective their current broker was, unfortunately, asleep at the wheel. I was in for a rude awakening. Instead of winning their business, I was told, "We're going to implement your suggestions. And I hate to tell you this, but we're not going to do them with you. We're having a discussion with our current broker. You need to understand that decisions are made for lots of reasons and this is a relationship decision. We're just not leaving our broker."

This was one of my greatest professional life lessons. I understand it very well now, and more and more all the time, as loyalty is very important to me personally. Loyalty is a dynamic that's important to a lot of business owners as well—especially small business owners—because they're not just analyzing data and spreadsheets to make their decisions. They are also putting faith in a particular person. And that can be a huge advantage for you. There's a significant difference when employers have known the broker they've been working with for years, versus when they're speaking with a voice on the phone who might be twenty years younger, or when they're receiving multiple emails day after day from a stranger trying to push information they have not asked to receive.

Let's return to the example of buying the sizzle instead of the steak. Most DTEs come in with the promise that they have simple software with great customer service and that you didn't really need your broker anymore. The truth, however, is very different. What happens when one of their customers calls into customer support and says, "Open enrollment is coming up. Who are you going to send out to meet with our employees to explain our benefits for us?"

Without question, their response will be, "We don't do that. We only work over the phone and online." How do you think that will go over? Or, let's say that an employee calls them with questions about their dental plan and needs to speak with someone. They will be put on hold and then transferred to the queue at their insurance carrier to wait for the next available customer service rep—with absolutely no help whatsoever from "their broker" at the DTE. All sizzle, but absolutely no steak.

That was the case with Zenefits, who realized that although they had great technology, being a broker is a full-time job. They hadn't built software to replace the broker relationship, just the benefits elections, enrollment, and management process. And, frankly, Zenefits didn't want to be the broker. So, they sold their book of business to OneDigital in 2017, and now they simply provide software solutions while partnering, to some degree, with other brokers. In the meantime, another very real threat to your business has since emerged— the former Zenefits founder, Parker Conrad, started a new company called Rippling. He is repeating the

Zenefits' playbook with a little twist on the story. And like Zenefits before, they are a direct threat to you.

So what is so special about DTE or PEO software that enables them to win small businesses from you? The seamless combination of payroll, HRIS, and benefits. Three functions with a single login and a database that is always in sync. I call this the Three-Legged Stool for small and medium-sized businesses.

Let's start with **payroll**. We know that payroll software for small businesses have been around for a long time, but as software solutions become more prevalent for employee benefits and other HR functions, businesses are weary of having to manage and train employees on multiple systems. Companies are looking for the systems to "talk to" each other, ensuring business owners and HR teams only have to make changes in one system, for them to be reflected in the other. We also know that payroll software is complicated and businesses typically only switch when they have a problem or bad experience. Messing up employee pay can cause a huge headache. DTEs and PEOs offer all-in-one solutions; but to benefit from that, businesses need to use the full suite of software they offer. Your opportunity is to "build" and pitch your groups on using systems that offer the best experience at the right price but *integrate* with each other. An integration solves the duplicate data entry headache businesses have, and why they might choose an all-in-one solution, while enabling them to work with the best-in-class solution for each of payroll, HRIS, and benefits.

The second leg of our stool is **HRIS**. Human resource information systems are becoming much more popular—even in smaller companies—because of increased regulations and the expectations of employees, particularly the growing Millennial workforce. PTO tracking and time-off requests are important features to be baked into an online tool or system and cannot be overlooked. Moreover, these solutions aren't just available online, but have mobile apps. Fifty-seven percent of the population uses mobile as their primary means of access to the internet and that number will only continue to grow.

The third leg of our stool is **benefits administration**. When I was a broker, I would go out and conduct employee meetings, always leaving behind a packet of kits for the group administrator to add new employees and manage changes. Now, employers expect holistic support—not just open enrollment management—as well as assistance for new hires, changes, and terminations.

DTEs offer an all-in-one solution that handles these changes easily and seamlessly online, which means you must be able to do it too in order to continue to compete for your small business clients.

For you it's all about maximizing the power and credibility that your trusted relationship with your customer affords you—a relationship that you have worked many years to cultivate. Combined with a technology solution for your clients makes you a fierce incumbent.

Part 4

It's Time to Be
a Digital Broker

What exactly do I mean by digital broker? Simply put, if you have adopted a technology solution to better serve your clients, if you have empowered your customer relationships by providing a complete suite of HR and benefits with Software as a Service (SaaS), if you have created an online presence for your business, have promoted that business through digital marketing, if you have sought to improve your client communication tools, and have streamlined the employee experience for your groups so that they can manage their benefits online, then *you* are a digital broker.

We will dive into what it means to be a digital broker in more detail, but first, let's return for a moment to you, a broker who is still tied to paper. Do you remember my scenario from the beginning of the book, the one that showed a typical day in the life of my time as a broker? This time, let's make it about you.

Let's say that you have a fifteen-member group, and it's time to re-enroll their medical, dental, and life insurance. You go to your storeroom and grab fifteen medical forms, fifteen dental forms, and fifteen life insurance forms. You collate them, type a memo, hop in your car, drive across town, and walk in to physically deliver them to the group. You then follow up with their administrator every few days. "Are the forms done? No? Okay, I'll call again later."

Then, the next call might go something like this: "Are the forms done yet? No? I understand that you're busy. We've just really got to get these forms done." Finally, once the group administrator gives you the green light, you once again hop in your car, drive across town, and pick up the forms. After you've checked in on your group and exchanged pleasantries, it's back into your car, where you traverse once more across town and make your way back to the office.

You then spend half a day proofing the paper forms. By the time you are done, you are practically seeing double. You inventory all the missing information, cross-referencing and double-checking as you go.

Then, you spend the next several days calling employees to gather their missing information. Sometimes, you get lucky and an employee picks up the first time you call; more often than not, that's simply not the case. Finally, once you have tracked down all of the missing bits and pieces, you finish completing all the forms, scan them in one by one, and submit the completed forms to the insurance carrier. It is exhausting just to think about.

But, what happens once you become a digital broker? To start, if you invest in the right benefits admin software solution today, you can learn how it works in about an hour. Imagine that—one hour of learning and all of those previous hours spent paper-chasing suddenly just goes away. Today's employees—regardless of group size—have certain expectations about their online experiences. This extends to their benefits experience as well. Today's employees expect to be able to click a link that brings them to a secure site, where they only have to fill out their name once, and where they can quickly and easily pick the benefits they want. They expect the system to automatically calculate their payroll deductions as they go through enrollment, because it already knows how old they are, using the rate tables as it calculates. They expect that the technology will work for them in a seamless and intuitive way, and they will apply pressure to their employers to extend this experience to them through whomever they partner with.

The ability to generate quotes is extremely popular, given the significant volume of time that goes into quoting rates before a broker can even begin enrolling a group. A digital broker can quickly quote groups and then use the same data from the sold quote to set up employee enrollment with only a few clicks. That means you will never have to go out for quotes again. When thinking about digitizing your business, it's wise to consider the sum total of each manual process or analog touchpoint. Is there a way in which to shift that behavior online in order to become faster, leaner, more nimble?

Continue to imagine that while all this is going on, you can quickly and easily check your groups' progress from your cell phone. You can see which employees are finished, who hasn't started, and who might have questions. You can even send an email notification to those who have questions or need help—right from your own device. And then when they are done, you can get a notification that their enrollment is complete. The digital broker can send enrollments directly to carriers through a connection with the carrier's database, getting ID cards into the hands of employees faster.

You can transform what had been an average of fifteen to twenty hours of work into less than thirty minutes. And the time investment you needed to put in to learn how to do it? It was at most, one to two hours. Right away, technology has made your workday exponentially easier and more efficient, which has, in turn, made you better able to serve your customers. And remember, when you factor in the power of loyalty and relationships, bringing the right technology solutions to your clients will help bulletproof your book of business against the threat of PEOs and DTEs who can never best you in creating strong relationships with your clients.

Consider this: if you're a digital broker, you now have everything at your disposal that you need to help your customers. You go from being behind the times to having more advantages today than you've ever had before. Remember, it wasn't that long ago that only a large company could afford to buy the computers, maintain the software, and have technology departments needed to support and provide this kind of service. Thankfully, that is simply no longer the case, and you too can compete like one of these comprehensive digital brokers.

Your business can grow by adopting technology and combining it with your trusted advisor status—the relationship skills that have already made your agency successful. Obviously your clients like working with you. You've been in the business for ten, twenty, maybe even thirty years, and you have an impressive book of clients that produces an excellent source of revenue. You've done everything right. By adding technology, you will be in the perfect position, not only to build that moat to protect your book, but to take your agency to a completely new level.

Benefits and HR are merging and technology is the impetus for this convergence. A single point of entry is the beginning. Benefits and HR share common data elements that, without this technology, need to be duplicated over and over again. When you onboard an employee, businesses have to set up payroll, medical, HR, dental, life, 401(K), an HSA plan, and the list goes on. Every single one of these requires the employee to enter his or her name and address on every single form, which then needs to be managed and double-checked by the HR administrator.

The emerging digital brokers, particularly the ones who have adopted SaaS, have raised the bar by offering comprehensive, integrated solutions for their clients, finding quality, low-cost payroll vendors that aren't looking to become the BOR (Broker of Record) and that integrate with robust benefits administration software, and simple HRIS tools. Along with this, they include ongoing eligibility management—meaning adds, changes in terms—as part of their standard service offering. In 2014, your small groups weren't being cold-called regularly with these types of offers. Today, they are called on relentlessly, with the requirement that in order to get these features, they have to sign over the Broker of Record letter—effectively, cutting you out. PEOs and DTEs are a growing and very real threat. If you think your clients won't leave you for them when the time comes, think again.

Prior to COVID-19, out of the more than six million small businesses nationwide, fewer than 2% had adopted a full online solution. However, in response to the monumental events that took place on a global scale during the COVID-19 pandemic, the country saw a dramatic shift to small businesses quickly adopting online solutions to help them manage virtual work environments. I can tell you from experience: once a company goes digital, they will never return to paper again. Over the next five years, we're going to continue to see a dramatic shift in how benefits are managed, with a massive increase in the rate of adoption of online solutions. Eventually, we will see that all small businesses are going to adopt these solutions because they're becoming increasingly more available, affordable, and they simply make good sense.

Small businesses have been talking about moving online for some time, but where people often go wrong is in the scaling. Group size is a significant factor in how you roll out this transition to digital. I have talked to hundreds of brokers who describe how moving online created a lot more work for them. You may be confused by this—shouldn't incorporating technology instantly make life easier?

Well, we can think about it this way: If you go to Delta Airlines to take a flight from San Diego to Los Angeles, they're not going to put you on a 747. That's the jet they reserve for their LA to China direct flight.

No, they're going to put you on a small plane to LA, because they scale the solution to fit the need. When becoming a digital broker, you need to apply the same logic.

Most businesses are small businesses—76% of businesses in America have fewer than ten employees. So, most of the time you're going to be dealing with very small businesses with "micro-group" characteristics. These groups don't have big onboarding and HR demands like larger companies do, and will generally only touch the system during open enrollment, when onboarding a new employee, or when an employee has a qualifying life event. They're likely to have very simple benefit plans; for example, many companies with three or four employees only have medical plans available, and are generally going to be self-service for payroll. They're not ready yet to go all in on a payroll solution. So you're not going to need to work with an integration, and HR is not yet a major factor. In all reality, many small companies likely only informally track PTO, using a calendar, notepad, or an Excel spreadsheet to keep track of their employees' time off.

So for three out of four of your cases, you can plan on keeping it really simple. You're replacing the act of handing out those five paper forms with instead having a single login for employees to fill in their information digitally. And if you keep your setup and management of those groups to that, it will only take you about twenty minutes to one hour per case. With that in mind, you'll save about sixteen hours per case, all the while, creating an enhanced benefits experience for your clients and their employees, who are likely prone to believing that robust digital solutions are reserved for the bigger operations. Imagine the kind of loyalty that will help create, while shutting the door on competition.

ACA Compliance and Technology

If you have been a broker for very long, it's likely that your day-to-day work life has changed a lot over the span of your career. I know that for me, in the very early days of my career as a broker, I was heavily involved in helping employees with their claim issues. Back then, managed care was not as prevalent as it is today. It was more common that you would go to a doctor who wasn't necessarily part of a network, and insurance companies would manage claim costs using what's called usual and customary (U&C), or reasonable and customary (R&C).

The idea was that when you went to a doctor's office for a checkup, the plan would pay 100%. That doesn't mean the doctor could charge $1,000 for that checkup. The plan paid 100% of usual and customary charges. There were indexes that track these costs by zip code, by live claim data. So, by looking in your zip code, you could see that checkups could range in cost from $90 to $159, with the 90th percentile being $159. So if the charge for that checkup was $300 and the plan paid 100% of the 90th percentile, it would pay $159, not $300. The rest was between the patient and the doctor.

So, as a broker, I would help employees navigate and understand these kinds of issues. That was a significant part of my job. Another responsibility I faced was handling questions and problems that pertained to pre-existing conditions. At the time, all plans were underwritten for health risk, and in the past, were offered with limitations and exclusions, such as pre-existing conditions. A group of ten employees might include three people with pre-existing conditions on their backs, so their plan would have a back rider. In such a case, for the first twenty-four months under the plan, anything related to this specific back issue would not be covered. It was my job then to field the employee questions and concerns that came up as a result.

That element of the business has largely gone away and issues like Family Medical Leave Act and ACA reporting and compliance are now much more prevalent. However, small businesses are ill-equipped to deal with these complexities on their own. They need a trusted advisor to still serve as an advocate or guide. Many brokers, and payroll vendors, have and continue to use free compliance support as an entry point to win new business, and groups have increasingly come to expect it.

The Affordable Care Act has a requirement for employers to produce a form called a 1095. In addition to their W2, employees receive this 1095 form. This form has twelve boxes for the months of the year, showing exactly what months an employee was covered under the employer's plan. The ACA requires that employers offer an affordable plan. To be considered affordable, the plan cannot exceed 9.78% of the employee's W2 wages. So if the employee's annual income is $50,000, the plan can't cost them more than $5,000 for the year, or $400 per month. If the employee declines the plan, the IRS needs to know, because the employee then has to show proof of other qualified coverage or they will be subject to tax penalties.

Welcome to ACA compliance, which by now, you likely already know very well. How can technology help? A good technology solution will integrate with a business's payroll and track compensation. These solutions give businesses a dashboard that instantly shows them whether or not they are ACA compliant, as well as which employees might have passed a threshold and require benefit plans. Then at the end of the year, the platform provides the data file, produces and fills out all of the 1095s, and prints them for the employer.

Becoming a digital broker means using technology to solve a variety of your clients' problems, enhancing your status as their trusted advisor and shutting out competitors that might use these challenges as an entry point.

Digital Security

We've all seen the headlines over the last several years: major companies, including some in the healthcare space, in the terrible position having been exposed by a data breach. Rightfully, brokers, employers, and employees are all asking the same question—are the technology solutions emerging in the benefits enrollment space secure? Brokers want reassurance that the confidential information their groups entrust to them is totally secure, as well they should.

The answer is yes, as long as you make sure that the technology you choose has adopted appropriate measures. The company should follow Cal data privacy

regulations, be HIPAA-compliant and have successfully completed a SOC 2 type 1 audit. Beyond that, all
data should be encrypted with industry standard AES-
256, both at rest and in transit. All brokers, employer
administrators, and employees of the technology provider should be required to use two-factor authentication for secure access. Finally, all data uploaded should
be scanned for viruses and malicious programs.

The fact is that you can never be 100 percent
secure, which is why monitoring is just as important
as protecting. Secure technology platforms run regular
assessments, including vulnerability and penetration
testing from third-party vendors, as well as routinely
undergo audits and reviews to ensure the most up-to-
date practices are being applied. All data access and
system changes should be tracked and those changes
should be stored securely.

Security has to be taken seriously, which means
requiring employees of the tech provider to follow
strict security procedures. Before an employee is
hired, a background check should be conducted. All
employees should complete monthly security training
and an annual HIPAA review, with access only given
out on an as-needed basis. Additionally, that access
should require complex passwords they are forced to
change regularly.

Something I mentioned briefly above was two-factor authentication, often referred to as Multi-Factor
Authentication (MFA). You may have experienced
your bank or credit card vendors requiring this commonly today. When you attempt to login to your
account, you must enter a code that you receive via
text. I share this example for a couple of reasons. First,

like many reading this, you may not have necessarily known what "Multi-Factor Authentication" meant—at least not in a practical way for your needs—so like you may with many technology discussions, perhaps you bypassed that section quickly. However, after a brief explanation in basic terms, you know exactly what it is. More often than not, you will find that many of the things you perceived as being "too complicated," will quickly become second nature.

We All Benefit from Going Digital

There are huge national brokers that have thousands of small groups with hundreds of thousands of employees. Then there are brokers—maybe like you—who might sell some life insurance, disability, property casualty and have twenty small groups within the community.

Offering a technology solution is also about the group's needs, not just broker's needs. When a broker loses a group, whether an independent local broker or a national broker, it's usually because the new broker provides a service or fills a need that the incumbent broker didn't offer. When I began the technology journey, I often was told, "My clients prefer paper; they aren't into technology." Through the years, I can't tell you how many times those same brokers, large or small, learned too late that it was really them, not their client, that preferred paper.

The nation's top agencies have a lot at stake too. Their books of business may generate hundreds of millions of dollars in revenue and they might have twenty thousand small business clients with more than a million employees. But they are no different than anybody else out there. They have the resources and the wherewithal to compete in a different way than the kitchen table broker does, but all the groups that they have are just as vulnerable to the DTEs, including payroll vendors, the PEOs, and new, digital brokers that are coming down market. Whether you're a big broker or a small broker, these channels are a direct threat.

If you've got a book of small businesses, all of these competitors run the same playbook, which is a technology-enabled, all-in-one solution aimed at picking off your small business clients one by one. If you are a small broker, they promote that you are too small to offer great technology. If you are a large broker, they may point out you are part of the "old school" and, while massive, slow as a cruise ship to turn with the times.

If I'm a $250,000-a-year revenue broker and one of my larger groups has one hundred employees and they generate $60,000 of my annual income, that's exactly the type of group I desperately one to keep. Well, unfortunately, that's the kind of group that my competitors want too. They like the $60,000 groups better than the $600 groups, just like I do. So let's say I do nothing to protect against this emerging threat and one day I get an email saying that my client signed a broker-of-record letter over to a competitor, making the competitor their new broker. Starting June 1, I will no longer get that $5,000-a-month check. That's a major impact to my commission. Perhaps if you're a broker whose business is constantly growing, the impact might not feel so great. But if you're not regularly adding new business, and you unexpectedly lose a group that may be one of the hardest of all to replace, well, that's a big blow.

In 2014, a broker who was not online might occasionally lose a piece of business to a DTE or PEO; today's brokers are losing clients much more quickly, which is why successful brokers are making the digital transition today. Like with any new technology, you will see an adoption curve: you have the early adopters, those in the middle, and those who wait until it's too late.

To add one more category to check in the pro-technology column, it is also green. Assuming that you are compliant, with the myriad of forms associated with the average annual renewal, a typical group consumes more than two hundred pages of benefits documentation every year per employee! That means a forty-two-employee group consumes an entire tree every single year.

By 2025, virtually all businesses will convert to technology. In the wake of the mass adoption that took place in early 2020, the real question is no longer if, but when and from whom they will buy it. Add the COVID pandemic of 2020 and the notion of face-to-face meetings, large group meetings, and paper forms being an accepted practice is quickly becoming history. You, their broker, must be ready to help them make the technology transition. *Too late* is coming very soon.

Part 5

The Digital Age Playbook

So now that you've read the previous chapter on becoming a digital broker, you have bought in and you're ready to go. You are thinking, let's get started. But how do you proceed?

1. Digital marketing is key. The first thing you need to do is establish your online presence with an effective website and social media pages, then dialing up your online outreach via email and social media.
2. Next, you must select an online enrollment solution that you can implement quickly with a few key groups to get up and running.
3. Evaluate payroll and HR solutions integrated with the online enrollment solution you chose in step 2 that you can recommend to your clients when they ask—as some already are and more will likely very soon—so they don't choose someone trying to cut you out of the equation.
4. Expand your benefit offering and increase commissions by offering additional ancillary coverage, benefiting from how much easier a software solution makes adding plans for a group.

5. Put all your groups online and remove technology as an advantage or talking point for your competitors. The quickest way for a technology-enabled broker to open the door is to talk to one of your customers that is not using technology.

Creating a Digital Marketing Strategy

And just how important is it today to market your agency? It's essential. You have to put yourself in front of your customers and your prospects, so they know who you are and what you can do for them. You can build an excellent offering, but it doesn't help if you don't tell people about it. Whether you realize it or not, your online presence—or your lack of online presence—has a serious impact on the growth of your agency. This is an irrefutable fact of doing business today.

The reality is that growing and thriving businesses have a digital presence, and dying businesses simply do not. You might not like hearing it, but I think by now we all know it's true. The question is, what's the message that you want to send your customers and prospects, those Millennial buyers, who, *to repeat*, will account for up to 75% of the workforce in just a few short years. Part of the remaining 25% will be the new GenZ right behind them. Every year we move forward, the world is more, *not less*, digital.

Today, Millennials make 60% of their total purchases online.[5] This largest generation in American history has already shifted the way we do business. In

_____

[5] https://couponfollow.com/research/millennial-shopping-report

the B2C space, we see that it is critical for companies and brands to exist digitally if they are to survive. But consider this: 63.3% of US executives will be eligible to retire in the next five years. If that holds true, then that leaves a significant leadership gap that will have to be filled by Millennials. Whether as an individual consumer, or in a business decision-maker role, you can count on one thing: Millennials will not engage with companies that seem behind the times. If they are used to experiencing their day-to-day life as part of an online ecosystem and your company doesn't have a meaningful online footprint, you will be deemed irrelevant. We are beginning to see it already as the tides continue to shift. Today, customers are already comparing solutions online. They will google you and your competitors before you even show up for an appointment. So if you have a consistent online presence that puts you in front of your customers digitally, it allows you to keep them informed, and in turn, allows you to stay relevant.

If this feels new or daunting, there are a few really simple steps you can take today that will help you bridge the gap between analog and digital marketing for your business. For starters, you and your business will be searched for online. What will customers and prospects find when they search for you on Google?

One great—and free—tool available through Google to help you manage how your business appears in the search results is Google My Business. You have probably encountered many examples of businesses using this online tool without even realizing it. When searching on Google for a specific business, have ever noticed the profile that pops up on the right side of the screen? For example, if you type the name of your favorite restaurant into Google, perhaps you have seen a description, address, hours, menu, phone number, and reviews from different platforms? This was likely done through Google My Business.

The process to sign up and verify your insurance agency in Google My Business is straightforward.[6] Once you follow the simple steps to enroll, you can take advantage of this tool to stand out when an HR professional looks online for a health insurance broker. In addition, Google My Business will help you understand your customers better by providing analytics on how visible your brand is and how users are engaging with it. By implementing Google My Business for your insurance agency, you will increase your website's traffic and edge out your competitors.

If you do not have a website, or if it is sorely out of date, step one is to solidify that next critical touchpoint. Thankfully, today you don't need to have experience in coding or web design in order to have a modern and easy-to-navigate website. Numerous options exist that make building your website not only easy but affordable—and in some cases, free. While you will have to purchase a domain name (that refers to your website URL) and pay for hosting, there are a lot of good options available to build and maintain your website. Some notable options include Wix, Squarespace, and WordPress.

---

[6] https://support.google.com/business/answer/6300717?hl=en

Regardless of what you choose, be mindful to look for the following things when evaluating a website provider:

- *Mobile Responsiveness:* Millennials are on their phones now more than ever before, and we have seen a 20% increase in online shopping from this group in the last eighteen months, surpassing desktop as the primary platform.[7] How does your website look when being viewed on a tablet or cell phone screen? Make sure that you have a mobile responsive site that adjusts and scales appropriately when a non-desktop browser is being used.
- *Templates and Customization:* A good website builder should offer plenty of templates for you to build out your company's website. However, ease in customization is also going to be important. Can you upload images easily? Are you able to change colors, fonts, etc.? Can you add pages or adjust icons? The point is that you want something easily customizable so that your company's page doesn't look like everyone else's.
- *Image Library:* On average, pages with images or videos draw **94%** more views than their text-only counterparts.[8] If you have done the hard work of getting prospective customers to your website, do not lose them by having text-heavy pages. You will want lifestyle images and

---

[7] The Millennial Shopping Report 2019 | CouponFollow
[8] http://hubspot.com/marketing-statistics

visually appealing graphics to keep them engaged on your website. However, most stock photography comes at a price. The last thing you want to do is google an image, download it, and then use it on your site. You will be slapped with a bill for copyright infringement. Instead, look for a website builder with a robust (and ideally, growing) image library. This provides you with the assets you need to keep your website looking clean and modern, while protecting you from unexpected costs around images.

- *SEO Features:* Search engine optimization sounds daunting, but in simple terms, it is baking in the right keywords to your content so that your site shows up on Google and Bing. That's it. Look for a website builder that makes SEO simple so that your pages will be more visible to search engines. There should be fields for image tagging, meta descriptions, title tags, etc. You don't need to be an expert on any of this—you just need a website builder that will walk you through the steps each time you add new content to your site.

- *Social Sharing:* When your website is up and running, you will want to be able to share and promote it! Ideally, you want it to be easy for your visitors to share and promote it as well. With the right sharing functionality, you can easily share a new post to your company's Facebook or Twitter pages. It will also make it easier for your visitors to share on their own social media accounts with just the click of a button. Look for site builders that make the image preview of your site look good when sharing it on social media. We've all seen blurry or incorrectly sized images when someone shares a website on LinkedIn or Facebook.

The criteria above are important to consider, regardless of the route you choose to establish your website. For many, simply hiring a professional service to build your site—which is very common—will be the most efficient and cost effective. Just keep in mind that you're trading off the ability to quickly update your website to cater to a new need, like a change in legislation or a global pandemic. If you can, choose the path that enables you to build a website using a tool that makes it really easy to swap out images, videos, and content.

Once you've established your website, it's important that you create a social media presence for your business as well. Facebook, LinkedIn, and Twitter are free-to-use options that will provide you with yet another way to show up digitally, as well as keep you front-of-mind with your clients on an ongoing basis. Make sure you link back to your website from your social media accounts. Here are a few easy tricks to maximize your social media marketing activities:

- *Plan ahead:* Build out a monthly content calendar to help you stay in a rhythm of posting. Plus, planning ahead will help your messaging be more strategic and will save you time in the long run.
- *Time your posts:* While there's no one-size-fits-all approach to posting, there are some best

practices and norms you can keep in mind to help you get the most out of your activity. For example, the best days to post on Facebook tend to be Saturday and Sunday, which get 32% higher engagement, followed by Thursday and Friday with 18% higher engagement. Research suggests that the best times to post are 9 a.m., 1 p.m., and 3 p.m., with 1 p.m. getting you the most clicks and 3 p.m. getting you the most shares. Adversely, the best days to post on LinkedIn appear to be Tuesday, Wednesday, and Thursday, with the best times falling before and after work, at 7–8 a.m. and 5–6 p.m.[9]

- *More = More:* The more networks you leverage, the more engagement you will have. It's that simple. You should plan on Facebook and LinkedIn at a minimum, as these are broadly used channels that will likely encompass most, if not all of your prospective and current business clients. Facebook is better for smaller snippets of content, as well as images and infographics. Keep in mind that most people scroll through their newsfeed, rather than navigate to specific pages. Make sure that what you post is attention-grabbing and engaging. LinkedIn, on the other hand, can be a great space for long-form content, such as publishing articles or linking to white papers or reports that you find interesting.

---

[9] https://coschedule.com/blog/social-media-best-practices-for-business/

- *Quality over quantity:* While you want to post as much of your own free content as you can to help you show up on the social media channels you employ, keep in mind that over-posting for the sake of it will make you less relevant and could lose you followers. It is more important to share the right content that is tied to your goals and objectives than to become a noise machine that just cranks out posts for the sake of it. There is no faster way to lose followers than to become a nuisance.
- *Make your brand personal:* Increasing, consumers are looking to people and not companies on social media. Take T-Mobile's former CEO John Legere, who's personal social media accounts represented the company. You're a small business's trusted advisor and building your personal brand by posting authentic content from YOU can go a long way.

Like building your website, you will also find that by googling "digital marketing services" or "paid social media management" you can find services that will manage your social media for you on a monthly subscription basis.

Once you have established your website, along with the right mix of social media platforms, the next step is to create a mechanism for ongoing email marketing campaigns. If this is not something you are currently doing as part of your digital marketing strategy, it may seem confusing, or frankly, out of reach. However, much like creating a new website or developing individual social media accounts for your business, it is not only important, but likely easier than you think to begin utilizing email marketing. Research shows that for every $1 you spend on email marketing, you can expect an average return of $42.[10] If you have limited marketing resources or budget allocation, with that kind of ROI, email marketing is a tool you simply cannot afford to do without.

The data shows that 81% of SMBs rely on email marketing as their primary customer acquisition channel, and 80% rely on it for customer retention efforts as well.[11] What that means is that if you are not using email marketing to win and keep your book of business, you can count on the fact that your competitors—other digital brokers—are.

Do you want your customers to find out from a broker that began marketing online before you about the newest, the latest, and the greatest in creative health plan financing? Or, would you rather they hear about it from you so that they don't pick up the phone to call the competitor in order to learn more? Having email marketing as part of your marketing strategy will help protect you from these threats. And you can get started with a myriad of free or inexpensive platforms in very little time. Service providers like Mailchimp, Omnisend, or Sendinblue allow you to have thousands of subscribers, with very high daily and monthly send limits before you incur any cost. This means that you can get

---

your email marketing campaigns up and running, usually at no cost to you. Some things to consider when developing your email marketing campaigns include:

- *Make a good first impression:* Your business's introductory email, also known as welcome campaigns, have a wildly high open rate, with 82% being opened on average.[12] With this many people opening your first email, it is highly recommended that you use this to your advantage. Add in some useful information or an invitation for them to engage with you more.

- *Interactive emails:* If you think that you need to have tons of content in order to warrant sending an email, think again. In fact, reports suggest that adding videos to your email can increase click-through rates by 300%![13] Get creative with your content and find ways to maximize engagement through embedding videos.

- *Personalization is important:* The average email open rate is 20.81%. However, data suggests that personalized subject lines can get you up to 50% higher open rates on average.[14] Customize your subject lines and your greeting with individual names and there is a good chance you will see higher open rates for your campaigns.

---

[12] https://www.getresponse.com/resources/reports/email-marketing-benchmarks

[13] https://www.martechadvisor.com/articles/marketing-automation-2/personalization-and-optimization-will-be-the-focus-for-email-marketers-in-2017/

[14] https://www.getresponse.com/resources/reports/email-marketing-benchmarks

The stronger your digital presence and the wider the range of places you exist online, the greater the likelihood that you will pop up in searches for prospective business. What's more, the better chance you have at remaining relevant and being front of mind for the clients whose business you are trying to retain. Whether new prospects or current clients are looking online for the help they need, you want them to find you first. You can guarantee that your competitors already have a digital strategy. Your best chance of success will come from defining your own digital strategy and fighting back.

Choosing the Right Online Enrollment Solution

You have created a strong digital marketing strategy and now have an online footprint That will ensure you show up and show well when business owners are searching for help with employee benefits. Now you're ready to pick your technology solution for online enrollment and benefits administration.

The most important thing to remember is that you aren't just choosing a product for today. You're buying a solution for the challenges you may encounter tomorrow. This includes not just the unique business challenges you may face, but the challenges brought on by a rapidly changing landscape. Between 2015 and 2020, 87% of Millennials took on management roles, vs. 38% of GenXers and just 19% of Baby Boomers.[15] Millennials

---

[15] https://www.slideshare.net/Officevibe/20-statistics-about-millennials -in-the-workplace

are not just taking over in terms of sheer volume of the workforce, they are over-indexing against other generations in terms of assuming leadership and managerial positions, meaning they will increasingly more often take the reins for business decision-making. Why does that matter and how does that relate to selecting the right online enrollment solution for your groups? With these digital natives comprising not only the bulk of the workforce, but being in the driver's seat for evaluating key business partnerships, you cannot afford to be a paper broker any longer. DTEs are looking for any way to cut you out of the equation, and without the ability to get your groups online—and fast—you run the very real risk of being rendered obsolete.

That means that when you're looking at a software solution today, it's wise to try to discover exactly what that software looked like last year. If it has the same features then as it does today, don't buy it! That software isn't developing quickly enough. Remember, you're not simply purchasing a quick Band-Aid for getting your groups online. You are investing in a solution and a team that is looking into the future and can see the challenges you are going to encounter tomorrow. If you invest in a company that is built on yesterday's technology, you run the risk of also becoming yesterday's solution to your clients as well.

You can bet your groups will google the technology you're offering and read reviews from users online. It's paramount that the technology you choose to adopt shows well to your groups online.

The technology solution you adopt now should make their jobs easier right away. Employers will look to find solutions that streamline the onboarding process, simplify open enrollment, can save time, and will reduce opportunities for manual errors. Some suggestions of things to consider while evaluating potential solutions are:

- *Widely applicable:* Does the solution work for all your groups using paper today? If you implement a solution for a 25-life group that's meant for a 100-life group, you're going to find it too difficult to implement and maintain, killing some of the benefits. If you buy software only for your >100-life groups but have a 25-life group ready to go digital, you'll need to maintain two software solutions—an expensive headache for you.

- *Reduction in errors:* Aside from being time-consuming, environmentally unfriendly, and an indicator of being outdated or inflexible, relying on paper forms can also create errors—a headache for you and your clients. Make sure that the solution you select has a way to audit for discrepancies so that you can quickly (and accurately) manage your group's data.

- *Continuity:* Does the solution work with YOUR partners? You don't have to adopt technology on your own. From carriers, to general agents, to enrollers, there are technology experts in the insurance ecosystem that can help you get started and support the software over time. Choose a solution that's built for you to continue to work with your partners so you don't have to go it alone.

- *Cost to the employer:* Does the solution you're offering your groups come at a price tag to them? Is the cost and package flexible depending on group size? Or can you offer not only a way to get their employees' benefits online, but a digital solution that can help keep their bottom lines healthy? The more value you can pass over to your clients, the better chance you have of retaining them.

- *Carrier connections:* Does the online solution submit data directly to insurance carriers? Does it keep information in sync so employees and admins only need to make changes in one system for updates to be made to multiple carriers? If a connection isn't available to an insurance carrier, can the group still enroll entirely online?

- *Security and protection:* You've seen the headlines—major national brands brought to their knees as the result of a data breach. Now more than ever, it is critical that you only partner with companies that take security risks seriously. When evaluating these potential partners, ask yourself these questions—does this company follow Cal data privacy regulations? Are they HIPAA-compliant? Do they follow industry standards for data encryption? Do they require two-factor authentication for their software? Data security threats are evolving in real-time; are you evaluating a partner that is committed to evolving their protection of your data just as rapidly? If not, you are putting yourself and your clients at risk.

- *Looking ahead toward the future:* As I've started already, it is imperative that you look for partners in the digital enrollment space that are constantly looking to the future for ways to help you grow and protect your book. When evaluating offerings, look at what else exists that will help set you apart from your competitors. For example, is there an app? What is the mobile experience with this technology solution? Are there other tools available to help my clients, such as core HR functions that might be able to exist in one online experience? These are the tangential offerings that not only will help you keep your book of business, but can position you to thrive in a newly digital environment.

- *Ease of adoption:* The best tech solution will be really, really simple and intuitive to use—that simplicity should extend to you, your clients, and ultimately, the employees themselves. It should work the way *you* work and replicate what you used to do on paper, mimicking the actual flow of your current process. With the right solution, you should be able to learn how to use the basic features inside of an hour. The first step, the second step, and so forth should be extremely straight-forward, making it so that it's easy to replace what you are currently doing with paper.

- *Ongoing tools and support:* The software solution you choose should provide marketing support, including print and digital brochures, walk-through videos, and PowerPoint presentations to help you move all your groups online. It should offer assistance in digitizing your agency, along with tools to help your groups successfully use the technology. This might include lessons, digital marketing blogs, or instruction guides. Your new tool should help you run email-marketing campaigns to prospective clients and make promoting your business effortless through automation and drip campaigns sent to them from you, keeping you in front of your groups at all times.

- The technology you purchase should have exemplary customer support. Can you talk to a real person on the phone when you're in a pinch? Why buy software that you then have to support entirely on your own?

- *Ratings and reviews:* Leverage data to make an informed decision. Today, there is no excuse for locking into an agreement blindly. Look for the technology solution that is most highly rated by actual users. Websites like G2 connect you to independently validated user reviews to help you make informed decisions. Plus, you can read real reviews and testimonials that come from actual users, rather than from companies looking to persuade you to buy their products and services.

Your clients are watching you. As the market becomes saturated with technology solutions, give yourself the advantage. Don't be afraid to really test out each solution you are considering. The site should move quickly and very fluidly, and you should not have to wait very long between screens or ever find the site under repair. Again, don't forget that mobile is becoming increasingly more important, no matter how small your groups may be. If you don't have a mobile solution, someone who does, can and will step in with that essential feature—and rest assured, they will take those groups away.

Once you have made the decision to adopt a digital benefits enrollment solution and you have selected your technology partner, it's time to develop a strategy to get all of your groups transitioned. I advocate the following steps for everyone:

1. *Engage your marketing campaign to current customers so all are aware of your capability.* Any client you have that would like to be converted from paper to online should be a priority.

2. *Evaluate your high-impact carriers.* These are connected carriers that automate processing TALE (terms, adds, and life events) for you and your customer. There are a few national standards that typically have a measurable percentage of everyone's book of business. By converting these accounts early, you reduce more of the manual, paper-based administration processes quickly.

3. *Never miss a renewal.* You need to convert your book of business, and if one of the two scenarios above have not resulted in a conversion, do so at the time your group renews. Even if you have a predominantly 2–3-employee groups, everyone wins. Your Millennial client expects to be digital, and managing a few dozen three-life groups is way easier online than in file cabinets.

Once you have made the decision to adopt a digital benefits enrollment solution and have selected your technology partner, you might be tempted to wait to put each of your groups online until they come up for renewal. Suppose that you have had the same fifteen-employee group for the past ten years, and that they renew each September with a major medical carrier. You may be thinking that your client is not going to make any changes between now and September, so why do anything sooner? The anniversary date seems like a natural trigger.

However, let's say you have fifteen groups with a national carrier that aren't yet coming up for renewal. Well, these carriers are the very ones with whom your new technology provider hopefully has direct connections. This type of connection is brand-new, but if some of your groups are already pleased with this feature, why not give your other twenty groups the same advantage *right now* and streamline your own workflow in the process? Besides, if you wait until open enrollment, you run the risk of encountering other problems and headaches that are prone to happening during that time. Besides, do you want to leave a task with little margin for error to chance during a generally high-stress time of year?

Bear in mind that since you're very likely a small business yourself, your technology solution also needs to be affordable for it to be sustainable for you. When you commit to a subscription service, it's going to hit your credit card every month. It will immediately become an expense for you. If it's not affordable, no matter how interested you may be, it will not empower you to succeed in protecting and growing your agency online. So, if you do commit to a technology partner and make that investment, you're going to need to see value or a return on your expense very, very quickly. The best way to do that is to rapidly learn how to use the features that make what you're already doing that much easier. In that instance, you can immediately recognize the savings in both time and resources.

And perhaps most importantly, you want a solution that delivers *through* brokers, rather than partnering with those who conduct their business by edging brokers out. As I already said, you know your clients better than anyone else and you have a strong, solid relationship with them. So the technology partner you choose should build upon and enhance that relationship with your client, not replace it.

One of the changes I've witnessed over time is the "partner" who plays both sides of the fence. Their solution advocates "bring your own broker" but they also offer brokerage services themselves—AND if their brokerage services are used, other services are discounted. Over time, and through management changes at your client, such an arrangement is risky, particularly when the business strategy of these entities is to eventually have everything in one place and expand their revenue into medical plan commission.

Through the years, I have encountered some brokers who have said that they are all set because they already built their own software solution. The truth is that while that might have been very impressive ten or twelve years ago, today, Millennial group administrators spend all day actively experiencing the world through the lens of the newest, the slickest, and the fastest sites. They will flow from engaging with Apple to Amazon and then into Facebook or LinkedIn within a matter of minutes. Everything they do, everything they were raised on is digital. And they can tell in five minutes which online solutions were built this year and which have been sitting unchanged for the last five years. Trust me when I say that once you lose credibility with this group, you will be hard-pressed to gain it back.

If you want to deploy technology, you have to embrace it, not just implement it. Anyone who embraces technology will never go back to the old way of doing things. Think of the way that the global economic landscape shifted following the events of the Coronavirus in 2020. Once consumers became accustomed to ordering groceries online, how many reverted back to the old way of shopping brick and mortar stores? Similarly, how many employees got in the habit of Zoom meetings or learned how to leverage tools like Slack during the disruption of COVID-19, only to revert back to days filled heavily with in-person meetings and face-to-face interactions? It's a fact of human nature that the brain will naturally migrate toward whatever behavior comes most naturally, meaning whatever is the easiest is what we will default to. When technology has been introduced and replaces manual, paper, archaic ways of business, I promise you, your groups will never go back. Either they will stay with you and go digital through the solutions you bring them, or they will leave you for a DTE or other digital broker who has gotten there before you. There is simply no other outcome.

Keep in mind, you can't simply buy a technology solution and then just selectively deploy it because you think you are being threatened by a competitor. If that's the case and you're going up against the DTEs, you will never be able to pull it off. They are professionals who come prepared to win against you and other brokers like you each and every day. You can't one day decide to hop down from the stands and field a pitch from Mariano Rivera just because you went out and bought a jersey, a bat, and a ticket to the game. If you want to win against your biggest competitors, you have to be prepared to play at their level. According to a recent article by SHRM, there are an unprecedented number of enterprise system vendors, benefit "point" solutions, and total benefit outsourcing providers to choose from in today's market.[16] In this high-stakes, extremely competitive environment, do you have a digital benefits enrollment solution that supports brokers? If not, the health of your business is at stake.

Agency Management Systems

When I was just getting started with my brokerage in Minnesota, we didn't have technology like brokers do today. And we certainly didn't have Agency Management Systems (AMS). I remember we had to do everything the hard way, paper and pen—and rolodex. At Ease, we're fortunate enough to have several quality partners not only in the AMS space but in other impactful areas like payroll, telemedicine, TPAs, and so much more.

---

[16] https://www.shrm.org/resourcesandtools/hr-topics/benefits/pages/selecting-benefits-providers.aspx

Becoming a digital broker today means using simple technology to make your job easier. And some of that begins by considering the use of an Agency Management System, which can help simplify your day-to-day operations at your agency.

If you are not familiar, an AMS is a SaaS technology that agencies use to more effectively run their operations and organize their book of business. Agency Management Systems can be built for specific niche markets within the insurance industry, like life and health or property and casualty. Think of an AMS as an industry-specific CRM that helps you organize prospects, clients, policies, agents, carriers, commissions tracking and processing in a way that makes sense to you—all while facilitating various workflows beyond sales. This software is designed to help organize your working processes and keep everyone on the same page.

AMS vs. CRM

Most brokers rely on a CRM for things like sales calls, relationship management, email integration and marketing, documents and more. So how does an AMS stack up comparatively? While CRMs used to be a must-have, it quickly became apparent these were generic systems built to adapt to the needs of various industries. Agency Management Systems are an insurance industry game-changer—and they're better than CRMs—because an AMS is built specifically for the insurance industry. The totality (all-in-one system) and productivity offered by a modern-day AMS is without equal.

Becoming a digital broker is never a happy accident. With that in mind, some of the most successful agencies will tell you their secret to improving business operations is their AMS. So, what are the benefits of an agency management system? For starters, with an AMS, you can manage your agency from anywhere:

Centralize your data and organize clients, prospects, groups, policies, agents and carriers all in one place. Your AMS serves as a single source for information (including emails) which can be backed up to avoid the risk of losing information.

Improve documentation without having issues duplicating information or looking up previous documents. Now, the same customer information can be viewed from every employee's desk.

Automate your workflow and spend less time on manual, tedious tasks and more time focusing on winning new business or providing better service to your clients. An AMS will allow you to create some automated workflows to do things like assign tasks to agents when a due date nears, send emails to clients when a renewal date is coming up, and send emails to prospects to stay top-of-mind.

Eliminate duplicate data entry, loss of productivity, and having too much data in too many different places. An agency management system is built to simplify and house data in a single place where everyone can view the same information.

Grow your book of business with an AMS by selling additional lines of coverage other than simply health insurance (property and casualty, auto, Medicare, Life, etc.); all of these lines can live within your AMS. You can also use this technology to get quotes, move a book of business, identify opportunities for cross-selling in addition to other sales opportunities.

Improve your profitability and professionalism by freeing up your team's time and allowing them to focus on providing better service to your clients. As you know, with more operational efficiency comes more profitability.

So, what are the unique features of an AMS? While the benefits of using an AMS are plenty, there's even more that helps further set this software solution apart from an ordinary CRM:

Integrate with 3rd party applications like Outlook, Word, Excel, email, and voicemail. Communications are able to be tracked in your AMS, and you can also create templates for commonly used customer letters to save you time from recreating frequently used communications.

Connect your data and view performance in real-time. See company information, plan details, group numbers, employee details, dependent details, and more. You can then utilize various reporting capabilities based on criteria you set.

Run the agency side of your business with an AMS that does it all. Technology tools to run the agency side of your business will free up your time, save you money, and organize your agency.

Using an AMS with Ease

Today, digital brokers who use Ease have access to any one of Ease's many AMS integrations. The beauty of this is that as a benefits administration system, Ease securely stores all of your groups' benefits data while your AMS is crucial for commissions tracking, agency-wide reporting, and more. Digital brokers who use one of Ease's AMS integrations no longer need to manually input data in both Ease and their AMS to complete reporting tasks. It also enables them to quickly and accurately audit all of their commission checks without manually verifying each enrollment, as well as easily understand where specific benefits are popular, and monitor compensation by carrier, client, or product line.

Above all, you want all of the technology you use to simply work well and work together. When evaluating your choices for AMS and online benefits administration, keep in mind a few non-negotiables that you should look for:

Keeping all of your data in one place

A modern agency often requires different technology tools to meet client demands and achieve revenue goals. If you have the right ben admin tech in place—one that enables AMS integrations—each tool doesn't have to be siloed from one another. After a quick setup process, you should be able to sync plan, enrollment, group, and employee data from your ben admin tech system to your AMS, eliminating duplicate data entry. Any groups created in should also be automatically created in your AMS.

Insightful and impactful reporting

As a digital broker you know how critical it is for you to look for and identify benefit trends across all of your groups. Integrating your agency management system with your ben admin tech provides you with a holistic picture to help identify opportunities for growth (like adding lines of coverage to existing groups). Synced information to your AMS should also allow you to accurately audit your commission checks without manually verifying each enrollment, understand locations where specific plans are popular, and monitor your compensation by carrier, client, and product line. The right ben admin tech solution that integrated with your AMS will help you grow your business and retain your clients.

Technology and Voluntary Benefits

Once you've established your digital footprint, created a digital marketing strategy, and selected the right online benefits enrollment partner for your business, there are still other opportunities to expand your revenue by becoming a truly digital broker. Remember, if you have adopted a technology solution to better serve your clients, if you have empowered your customer relationships by providing a complete suite of HR and benefits with Software as a Service, or SaaS, if you have created an online presence for your business, have promoted that business through digital marketing, if you have sought to improve your client communication tools, and have streamlined the employee experience for your groups so that they can manage their benefits online, then *you* are a digital broker. Having the right technology in place will make your journey to becoming a digital broker feel effortless. Just imagine, when you hand out fewer forms, there is far less for your group administrators to have to track. That creates a seamless experience that opens the door to you being in a position to offer your groups additional benefits.

According to a study by Guardian Life Insurance Co. of America, "most employers have increased their spending on benefits-related technology in the past five years, with about half expecting further increases in the next three years."[17] The study went on to say, "Benefits technology is reshaping how employers think about their benefits strategy. A multi-generational workforce along with mounting pressures on employers to contain costs, simplify their benefits, and stay compliant are prompting employers to make this a priority." It's clear that the more opportunities you can create to strategically streamline HR processes while connecting groups and their employees with enhanced offerings, the more relevant you will remain for your clients. An easy way to help your clients add value to their employees while offering you additional revenue opportunities is through the expansion of voluntary benefits.

When I was a broker, copays presented two choices: an employee could have a $10 copay or a $25 copay, and perhaps a $100 deductible. It was unheard of to have a $5,000 deductible back then, whereas now, it is an unfortunate reality for many. Today, through that lens, it makes clear financial sense to fold in an offering of ancillary or voluntary products. When employees are faced with covering medical costs incurred from an illness or an accident, if they must first meet

---

[17] https://www.guardianlife.com/benefits-administration/study/digitizing-benefits-delivery

a $5,000 deductible—an amount that most people simply can't afford—they may find themselves financially in dire straits.

Given how important additional benefit offerings like ancillary and voluntary can be to employees, it makes sense that employers would place a higher value on the companies that can connect them and their employees to these types of expanded offerings. You can count on the fact that DTEs will try to sell your clients on more comprehensive benefit plans and that in many ways, they have the upper hand in doing so. Given that they aren't brokers, this is the only hand they can play to compete with you on benefits. The best line of defense in protecting your book of business against these interlopers is by putting expanded digital offering in front of your clients before they get the chance.

The average job tenure for a Millennial today is only two years, compared to five years for GenXers and seven years for Baby Boomers. What's more, it costs an employer an average of $24,000 to replace each Millennial employee that leaves their organization.[18] This dramatic turnover costs the national economy $30.5 million each year![19] What these startling figures should tell you is that if you can help your clients demonstrate better value back to their workforce—especially their Millennial employees—you can position yourself as not only a trusted partner, but an invaluable resource to help your groups approach benefits in a way that supports

[18] https://www.slideshare.net/Officevibe/20-statistics-about-millennials-in-the-workplace
[19] https://www.visix.com/resources/infographics/13-important-facts-about-millennials-in-the-workplace/

them in better retaining their employees. As a whole, Millennials are more inclined to embrace individuality; therefore, their expectations for their employer is that their personal needs can—and should—be met.[20] This means saying goodbye to a one-size-fits-all approach to benefits, offering more customization around plans, products, and services, and creating more pathways for employees to secure the voluntary and ancillary products they want and need.

We've gone through the numerous advantages that can be found both for employers, as well as for employees, when adding in expanded benefit offerings. What does it look like for you, however? You may be wondering what the downstream effect is for your business. I will tell you, adding in voluntary benefits as part of your digital broker offerings is a surefire way to increase your revenue. The average commission in the first year for a voluntary benefit product is about 40%—possibly higher. The average participation rate is also around 40%, depending upon whether or not it is assisted—in which case it's higher. If it is unassisted, you can anticipate that it will be a little lower. With all of that in mind, the average annual premium purchases on voluntary products is typically around $600. If your average case size is fifteen employees and you have thirty groups, this would generate an additional $43,200 in commissions for you—in one year alone. That is a **32% increase** over what you probably make on those groups right now. If you're an agency with three hundred accounts, averaging twenty employees

---

[20] https://www.honeybeebenefits.com/millennial-employee-benefits/

in your groups, that is more than $500,000 of additional revenue. If you are a digital broker offering a SaaS solution to your clients, you just have to turn the expanded offering on. Image—a 32% increase in revenue YOY (Year-over-Year) with just the click of a button. It should be clear to you that there is a reason DTEs or PEOs would want to steer your clients toward a similar comprehensive suite of benefit offerings. If you don't get there first, you will be leaving money on the table, possibly for good.

If you are still in a paper world, you know how cumbersome this new offering might be. You would have to go out to all your customers, have a meeting, and pass out yet another set of forms. That's just step one. All of the additional delays, wait times, and potential errors still apply. Even if there is additional revenue to be found, having these outdated, paper-driven processes in place creates barriers in both feasibility and time. Additionally, employees are weary about these options and how much will be coming out of their paycheck. However, if you have strategically moved your groups to an online solution, these barriers instantly disappear. Your groups and their employees will already be accustomed to the streamlined and user-friendly digital open enrollment experience each year. Now, when you incorporate a new voluntary or ancillary offering, it just looks like another button on their menu when employees walk through the enrollment process. If they need the product, they can buy it. If they don't, they can simply choose not to select it. It has truly never been easier for you—or for the DTEs or PEOs you are going up against—to turn on new revenue. Winning will look like whoever can get there first.

Planning Your Exit Strategy

Depending on where you fall within the continuum of your career, you may be particularly thoughtful right now about the value of your agency. If you are like me, you've spent your career building a business that not only provided for you and your family financially, but that gave you a sense of purpose, that helped support your local community, and that was intended to provide continued security and stability for you during your retirement years. So of course when the time comes, you will naturally want to exit at a premium— it's not just a matter of receiving fair compensation for something of intrinsic monetary value; it's a matter of ensuring that the legacy you've built is intact and that your years—perhaps even decades—of tireless work will now pay off.

Similar to defending and growing your business, simply having a healthy book and great relationships with your current customers is not enough to put you in a favorable position when you go to sell your agency. Today's buyers are looking to purchase agencies that can demonstrate to them that the business can continue operating without interruption and is optimized for future growth following the sale. If you don't know how you're going to eventually make your exit, know this—if you have been running your business without technology, chances are good that it's going to be very difficult to sell your business at all, let alone at the price it deserves. The sad reality is that in order to sell, you very likely may have to hand over the reins to your business at a significant discount. This can have devastating financial consequences, along with being very difficult to navigate from an emotional perspective. You should do everything you can now to prevent putting yourself—and your financial future—at risk in this way.

Let's say you have a $500,000 book of business. You probably have three service staff working for you for about $70,000 a year, yielding you a $290,000 annual net to your agency. We call that the EBITDA—which stands for a company's earnings before interest, tax, depreciation, and amortization—essentially, a measure of your company's operating performance without having to factor in financing decisions, accounting decisions, or tax environments. One thing you can be certain of is that when prospective buyers evaluate your business today, aside from just operational efficiencies and optimization opportunities, they will be looking at your cash flow and revenue favorability. Do you remember in the previous section when we talked about turning on new revenue through voluntary and ancillary product offerings? In that scenario, a conservative estimate of increased commissions from new voluntary subscriptions added 32% to your revenue YOY. When you start to think about selling your business, that additional revenue can be critical.

Today, the typical buyout on a small group at point of sale—depending on which region of the country you fall in—is about five times EBITDA. This means that in our scenario above, a broker who sells his business is going to exit at about $1,450,000 in profit.

Now, let's say you adopt technology and digitize your book. The 32% increase that you would be able to gain simply by offering your voluntary benefits to your group is only one stream of revenue available to you when you make the switch to becoming a digital broker. If you open up the marketplace, you can grow your entire book by another 20% easily. And with the efficiencies you derive from having your book online, you will be in a position to run it more easily and with fewer staff.

Your EBITDA just went up—way up.

At my company, we work with eight of the top ten brokers in the country. These brokerages are constantly in the process of acquiring new books of business. One thing I've learned is that if they can purchase a digitized book of business that uses the same system they use, allowing the groups to be transferred under their control, they are willing to pay much more. In fact, they will pay **seven to nine times** EBITDA, due to the ease of adoption and the low churn that comes from a smooth implementation experience. Now, simply by bringing your book online, you're suddenly looking at an exit payout of $3.2 million—more than doubling your profit!

There are a lot of things you can do to position yourself for success when it comes time to think about selling your business: going through a formal valuation process with an independent CPA, establishing a strong name and presence within your community, and having seasoned and knowledgeable employees—whether support staff, producers, or a mix of both. But the defining factor that will translate to real dollars will be whether or not you have truly become a digital broker, positioning yourself for a lucrative acquisition.

When I speak to a room filled with younger or more junior brokers, I know they're likely already using technology, or they're in the process of deciding what tool they're going to use. Millennials—even Millennial insurance brokers—are natives to technology; that's their world and they wouldn't consider working without it. In fact, 70% of Millennials admit to utilizing their own apps—even when it's against corporate policy—in order to be able to work more effectively.[21] This should come as no surprise. However, when I look at slightly more seasoned brokers who already have a solid business generating a large amount of revenue, I typically see that they need help finding efficiencies, though they are probably already infusing technology into their business to some degree.

But let's consider the average broker. Today, the average broker's age is about fifty-eight years old. Maybe this feels like you, or you know that it will likely feel like you before you know it. From this group—the average broker—what I constantly hear is, "It's too late in my career to do this. It's too late for me to make this change. I don't know how I would even start." If that sounds like you, I'm delighted to tell you that you are simply, flat-out wrong. In fact, if I've learned anything, it's that you are exactly the person who has the most

---

[21] https://www.slideshare.net/Officevibe/20-statistics-about-millennials-in-the-workplace

to gain from making the change to becoming a digital broker. And today, it has never been easier to start.

To put it in more relatable terms, when you are getting ready to sell your house, what do you do? If you're a savvy homeowner, you know that right before going on the market is the perfect time to invest some time and money and fix up your house. I remember doing this before selling our first home. That honey-do list that had grown and grown over the years suddenly transformed into our must-do list in order to maximize the profits for our little house. Looking back, even before we called in a realtor, we stepped back and thought, *Wow, the house looks better now than it ever has*. My only wish then was that we'd done it all sooner!

Ultimately, why did we fix up our house? Sure, we always knew that it would be nice to do this or fix that. But at the end of the day, we made the decision to tackle certain value-adding projects at that time because we knew we were going to be selling our house. Can you relate? When it is time for you to finally sell your business, you want to get as much money as you can, maximizing your profit. If you would apply that logic to selling a house, why wouldn't you do the same thing with your book of business? Mark my words, if you spend the next eighteen months actively and deliberately digitizing your business—no matter what the size of your book—it's going to yield you the biggest return on investment of your entire career.

Your customers are investing in you because they know you will deliver a solution for them today. My guess is that if they are still with you today, despite the DTEs and PEOs that are constantly circling around them, striving to snatch up their business, then it means that and more importantly—for now at least—they are also putting their faith in you to deliver tomorrow's solutions as well. To keep your clients in the face of unprecedented competition and increased risk, they need to be confident that you are already looking ahead, charting a course to help them navigate through the changes that will emerge tomorrow. They need to be sure that you will have the right solution in place for the challenges tomorrow will bring, even before you— or they—know exactly what's coming. Becoming a digital broker is essential to meeting your customers' needs today, *and* tomorrow. Luckily, becoming one has never been easier. So, isn't it time to get started?

Appendix

The Benefits Industry

The insurance industry is complex. There are a lot of moving parts, and unless you've been in the industry for over a decade or more, it's practically impossible to know everything.

I've put together some information about the insurance industry that will help you not only understand health insurance, but what Ease's ideal customers do and what they deal with on an average day.

What Is Health Insurance?

Health insurance covers the whole or a part of the risk of a person incurring medical expenses, spreading the risk over a large number of persons.

In the United States, employers usually contribute to healthcare. Applicable Large Employers (ALEs) are required to due to the Affordable Care Act. The average employer covers about 74% of a benefit plan, and the employee often covers the rest. Benefits are usually deducted from employees' paychecks.

Medical, dental, and vision are the types of insurance most commonly offered.

Health Insurance Is Offered Through Benefit Plans

Benefit plans are a collection of items or requirements. They usually include forms, employer contributions, employee contributions, rates, etc.

- Basic Information
- Eligibility
- Rates & Contribution
- Documents & Links

Networks - Benefit Plans

Medical and dental plans often have networks of "preferred providers" where an individual gets better benefits, or coverage by using providers in the network versus outside the network. It's rare, but some plans have no network.

The rationale behind using provider networks stems from agreements and practices that demonstrate a lower cost of delivering health care via best practices and competitive, discounted fee schedules.

Common types of network benefit plans:

1. **Open Access:** Go to any doctor you want, anywhere you like (these are rare now).
2. **Health Maintenance Organization (HMO):** The individual selects a Primary Care Physician (PCP) or Primary Care Clinic (PCC) and care begins there. The member always visits their designated

primary provider for care. If specialty care is needed, they are referred by their primary care provider.

For dental plans, these are referred to as Dental Maintenance Organizations (DMO) or Dental Health Maintenance Organizations (DHMO).

3. **Preferred Provider Organization (PPO):** Better benefits are received when using network providers rather than non-network providers. However, the member is free to use any provider in the network without referral to specialists.

   For dental plans, these are also referred to as Preferred Provider Organizations (PPO).

4. **Exclusive Provider Organization (EPO):** Similar to an HMO but typically an even smaller subset of providers that deliver the highest level of benefits for the lowest out-of-pocket fee.

Common Benefit Plan Components

Health benefits packages for employees are usually compiled of Core benefits AND Voluntary OR Worksite.

- Core are Medical, Dental, Vision, Short-Term Disability, Long-Term Disability, Life, and AD&D (Accidental Death & Dismemberment)
- Voluntary and Worksite are categorized according to whether rates are based on employer location or EE
  - Voluntary and Worksite = Life, AD&D, STD, LTD
  - Voluntary and Worksite CAN be included in Core; it depends on what the employer wants to offer/sponsor.

Core Benefits

Medical

Medical plans can vary widely in design. Ranging from those that cover most expenses with very little member out-of-pocket costs to those with very high deductibles.

- **Deductible:** Similar to auto insurance. The "front end" cost that the member is responsible for. Example: The plan has a $1,000 deductible. The member, therefore, pays the first $1,000 of expenses out-of-pocket before the plan begins to pay any benefits.
- **Copay or Copayment:** A defined amount paid by the member for a service. Common examples would be office visits and prescription drugs. A plan with this feature may have a $35 copay for an office visit. Or a $15 copay for prescription drugs.
- **Coinsurance:** The share of costs a member is typically responsible for, after the deductible or copayment. For example, after the deductible is satisfied, the plan pays 80% of expenses.
- **Out-of-Pocket Maximum:** The most a member is responsible for during a calendar year before the plan pays 100% of all expenses.
- **Over-the-Counter vs. Prescription:** Over-the-Counter are drugs you can by without a prescription (e.g., Advil).
- **Name Brand/Generic/Formulary/Name Rx:** Prescription drugs can fall into any of these categories. Health plans will usually pay a different benefit level for each.

- **Name Brand:** The original patented drug with a brand name. It's the most expensive and typically carries the highest copay and is often not covered if a generic is available. An example of a name brand over-the-counter drug is Advil.
- **Generic:** This is the black and yellow package. The generic for Advil is ibuprofin and typically labeled as Walgreens or CVS, and is much less costly. A generic is considered bioequivalent. The drug has the identical active ingredients and is tested to be consumed/absorbed in virtually identical ways.
- **Formulary:** A specified drug that receives a preferred benefit. This will be a drug that treats the same underlying symptoms but is not bioequivalent. It could be a brand name but may be generic. If a generic is available, it will typically be used. An over-the-counter example would be Tylenol and Advil. Both treat headaches but have completely different active ingredients (ibuprofen vs. acetaminophen).
- **In-Patient Hospital Services:** Services received while treated in a hospital and considered in-patient. This means the hospital has admitted you. As a rule of thumb, you are admitted if your stay is expected to last more than twelve hours.
- **Out-Patient Hospital Services:** Services received at a hospital but not as an in-patient. A common example would be a scheduled procedure at a hospital that is done the same day. Many of these services are now performed in an office setting.

- **Emergency Room:** The most expensive place to receive health care so typically plans have high out-of-pocket expenses associated with this level of service.
- **Urgent Care:** Specialized, extended-hour facilities that provide unscheduled care and after-hours care. Most emergency room services are redirected to urgent care. A common example would be a cut requiring stitches. While not life threatening (emergency room treatment), it demands immediate care.

The contribution of the level of service for each of the components above varies based on the benefit plan.

Dental

Dental insurance pays for services such as cleanings, fillings, and other dental care. Like medical plans, dental plans may have networks and work in a similar manner in terms of paying higher benefits when using preferred providers.

Dental plan offerings vary but generally follow a common theme around four categories of services: Preventive (not preventative), Basic, Major, and Orthodontia.

- **Preventive:** Cleaning, polishing, and scaling of teeth.
- **Basic:** Basic restorative services such as fillings (amalgam on anterior and composite on posterior); periodontal and endodontic (gum) care.
- **Major:** Bridges, crowns

- **Orthodontia:** Braces (almost always limited to children).

Dental plans usually have an annual maximum benefit of $1,000 to $2,000 per person.

A typical dental plan would be: 100/80/50/50 which would mean: 100% Preventive, 80% basic, 50% major and 50% for orthodontia.

Short-Term Disability (STD)

Replaces lost income due to an injury on a short-term basis. A common plan would be 60% of lost earnings up to a maximum weekly benefit of $500 per week for the duration of twelve weeks.

Long-Term Disability (LTD)

Replaces lost income due to an injury or illness on a long-term basis. A common plan would be 60% of lost earnings up to a maximum monthly benefit of $5,000 per month until age sixty-five.

Life and AD&D (Accidental Death & Dismemberment)

Pays a defined benefit in the event of death. Plans will commonly pay an additional benefit if the death is accidental. A common plan would be $50,000 of Life/AD&D.

Voluntary / Worksite Benefits

Life, AD&D, STD, LTD

These are plans that the employee can choose to buy at their own expense. The previously discussed benefits were either fully or primarily paid by the employer. Common voluntary benefits include:

- Life
- AD&D
- STD
- LTD

Employer-Sponsored versus Voluntary

- This is a mildly confusing concept but one to be aware of. It is important to be able to distinguish between them because their offerings and characteristics differ.
- The primary difference is:
  - **Employer-Sponsored:** The contract is technically a group contract and subject to ERISA laws such as COBRA (more on this later).
  - **Voluntary Benefits or VB is technically an individual contract and not subject to these laws.** A common VB provider is Aflac. VB Benefits include the above but also:
    - Critical Illness
    - Intensive Care
    - Cancer
    - Accident

Voluntary benefits allow employees to pick and choose. This introduces a concept known as Adverse Selection. For example, a ninety-year-old diagnosed with cancer and given three weeks to live is more likely to purchase and willing to pay more for life insurance than a healthy twenty-five-year-old. Therefore, voluntary benefits make the following adjustments:

- Age-Banded Rates
- Medical Underwriting for Higher Limits
- Limitations

ERISA (Employee Retirement Income Security Act of 1974)

ERISA was a comprehensive law that had a significant impact on Employee Benefits. Highlights include:

- A plan that follows certain rules is considered qualified. The benefit of being qualified is that an employer can deduct the cost of such plans AND the cost is not considered a taxable benefit to the employee. In addition, through a properly structured arrangement, employees can make their contributions toward plan costs on a pre-tax basis.
- Established rules for how benefits are offered. A plan cannot be discriminatory and maintain qualified status. ERISA has specific rules to determine if a plan is discriminatory.

COBRA (Consolidated Omnibus Budget Reconciliation Act of 1986)

COBRA requires that qualified plans extend the right for terminated employees and dependents to continue their health coverage for a predetermined period at their own expense. Generally, an employee can continue coverage for up to eighteen months. This is often referred to as Continuation.

Consumer-Driven Health Plans

As out-of-pocket costs and deductibles increase, more employees are required to pay for health care expenses out-of-pocket. There are a number of Consumer Driven Health Plan (CDHP) options for different purposes.

Flexible Spending Plan (FSA)

These are the original plans to allow employees to pay for expenses on a pre-tax basis. There are three primary types:

- **Health FSA:** Allows the individual to set funds aside for qualified expenses. You can google "Eligible FSA Expenses" and readily find current lists. These generally include items that would be eligible under your health plan but were subject to deductibles, copayments, or coinsurance. Additionally, the IRS has expanded the list to include some over-the-counter medications. The general requirements are that these are to treat symptoms of an illness.
- **Limited Health FSA:** This works in the same way as a Health FSA but has greater limits on additional expenses. This is designed to work in conjunction with an HSA (see below). If an individual has an HSA, the FSA is further limited so

it cannot pay for any MEDICAL or health plan expenses. It can pay for vision, dental, or other qualified expenses that are not eligible under the medical plan.

- The IRS periodically updates the maximum limits for FSA plans. In 2018 the maximum contribution was $2,650.
- Health FSAs also have a "use it or lose it" provision and elections cannot be changed without a qualifying event.
- **Dependent Care FSA:** This allows an employee to set money aside on a pre-tax basis for child daycare (most common) and certain adult dependent care expenses (e.g., if you are caring for an elderly parent).

The IRS has a maximum limit of $5,000 per year for dependent care.

Parking and Transit

There is both a Parking and Transit option that allows employees to set aside funds to pay for parking and transportation expenses related to work. The 2018 limit was $260 per month. This can be changed (unlike a Health FSA) and is reduced by any employer contributions made toward this expense.

Eligibility & Rates

Employee eligibility & rates (the cost that both the employer and employee pay) may depend on criteria such as (but not limited to):

Eligibility

- Part-time vs full-time
- The number of hours worked

Rates

- Health history
- Age
- Tobacco use

Index

NOTES

NOTES

NOTES

NOTES

NOTES

NOTES

NOTES

NOTES

NOTES

NOTES

NOTES

NOTES